T0314835

THE EASY LIFE

('La Vita Facile')

By Alda Merini

Translated by Camilla di Liberto

This book has been translated thanks to a translation grant awarded by the Italian Cultural Ministry of Foreign Affairs and International Cooperation.

Questo libro è stato tradotto grazie ad un contributo alla traduzione assegnato dal Ministero degli Affari Esteri e della Cooperazione Internazionale italiano.

Building futures, Bridging divides

The Easy Life
(La Vita Facile)

By Alda Merini
Translated by Camilla di Liberto

© 2018 Arkbound Ltd

ISBN: 9781912092512

First published in the original Italian in 1996 by Giunti Editore
First English translation by in 2018 Arkbound Ltd (Publishers)
Cover image by Emma Oliver

Arkbound is a social enterprise that aims to promote social
inclusion, community development and artistic talent. It
sponsors publications by disadvantaged authors and covers
issues that engage wider social concerns. Arkbound fully
embraces sustainability and environmental protection. It
endeavours to use material that is renewable, recyclable or
sourced from sustainable forest.

Arkbound
Backfields House
Upper York Street
Bristol BS2 8QJ
England

www.arkbound.com

THE EASY LIFE

('La Vita Facile')

Objects don't care at all about our life, yet we care a whole lot about the history of these wild beings who invade our mornings. These beings who wake up with us at dawn and who keep repeating cruelly: 'You're still here with us, alive once more.'

Adultery

A is for adultery. I, my dear, have never betrayed anyone, although I have wanted to. I consider sin the theological collection of my desires.

How many saints have changed their voices according to their thought, how many saints have corrupted their flesh to get to the focal point of truth.

With my conscience clear of sins, what else can I say about myself if not that I know life? I cultivate images; yours, for instance, which doesn't have a proper moment of glory. I cultivate passions for all the free time of my future.

Still I do not dare to sin.

I refrain from votive lamps like a shameful maiden who doesn't oil the light of her patience.

The phone numbers written on the walls were born out of tiredness, or maybe out of laziness.

At home pens are impossible to find; on the other hand, my friends have spoilt me so that I leave the heavier labours to them.

So then, since Spaini[1] has disappeared, I go to the café downstairs and observe the barista as he writes down the bills and the menu. I take revenge on the super-efficient Spaini writing down phone numbers on the walls with lipstick and stones found on the floor.

Picasso used to do the same. Since they didn't let him draw, he would stain clean sheets with fresh paint, so that they started calling him retarded and possessed. Geniuses, young and old, have always done odd things.

As Giotto's famous 'o', which left Cimabue astounded, my first line of poetry, written on a blackboard with chalk, was noticed by everyone too. I was equally taken by the awe and I began to think myself a poet.

---

[1] Guido Spaini, editor of the Italian version of the book.

Amazon

My heart is a piece of ice which reflects your beautiful face.

If it weren't of pure crystal then you wouldn't be able to admire yourself in it, my everlasting Narcissus. In you I have seen a maiden and a cittern.

It is told that the man became virtuous when he picked up the cittern which surely belonged to a woman. Women only could touch art with bewitching hands.

Thus the wonderful Orpheus dove his beautiful face in the water. He came out of it too effeminate and short-sighted to see the Furies, gems of pure hatred, commas of darkness.

There was a fear at the dawn of this mystery. There was a hand that suddenly became incandescent and lyrical. A hand that wished to touch that half-human, half-divine shoulder too.

Humans are such that they want to ascertain God's presence. Yet that cannot be done, since Love is hell, yet it is a tall church barrier too. You need clever horses to jump this double wall, you need beautiful thoroughbreds.

I need you; you fiery, rebel, one-breasted Amazon; you who freely fires the bow of purity. How beautiful you are in your staying.

Tell me then, if there is any difference between you and Narcissus, between the lonely waters of destiny and your tall mountain of purity. Oh prodigious alp, whose lip dies out, vanishing in a wide smile. You are not of this Earth, you are an exceptional vision, a miracle of the mind. Sultans resemble you, servants resemble you, all things becoming resemble you. Yet you cannot touch the earth.

If I could catch you, Chicca[2], I would soil you as I am soiled with good earthy sins; I would smear you with my own mud. Then you would be a sinner goddess.

Though sin does not suit you. Then you wouldn't be clothed in such dress that violates the air, that inebriates even your own skin. You wouldn't be running free of revenge. You wouldn't have those big eyes ringed with life.

Death cannot touch you, as you do not sink into the abyss like Orpheus, you do not crave love, you began before love and will follow it through. You forget all, despite being born wonderfully beautiful.

---

[2] Chicca Gagliardo, editor of the Italian edition of the book, together with Guido Spaini.

Angels

I was thinking that angels don't have desires, yet it's curious how they want to inhabit humans and understand how they live, how they play with love and how they go to school to learn how to die.

Angels live among us every day; many shifts of memories and objects, much confusion is raised by their joyfulness: they are soaked in candid wine, they wear puffy dresses like fairies do and they calm God's anger with their tapered hands.

They busy themselves with many things, wandering around harlots and reprobates, saints and health enthusiasts, trying to sort out that mishmash of words that give life to people and get them all confused instituting Babel towers new and old.

Angels solve everything, with melody, with music, the only true universal language.

Yet I also know wood is the symbol of memory and that it lets out others' love and goodness. Keeping our hands nailed to the wooden benches of the asylums would muffle the swift, sudden message of our thoughts.

Until one day such aggression of thoughts and those wooden benches became gigantic like cacti, sliding like rosaries.

Tears of love fell on those plants, as tears of love fall at the end of great relationships, when passion, so strong and fleeting, has snapped in two anxiety's sword and has forever broken the certainty that the ego is untouchable.

Only after love, when we have been emptied of all doubt and fury, we look into each other's eyes with attentive desperation and we cry, realising that a love so deep must die with us.

Harp

Greetings to you too, Ariadne; actually no, to you, Daphne the pure. I saw you, covered in see-through veils, playing the Aeolian harp.

You inspired me too; without you, great liar, yet beautiful, I would have never started to sing.

They say it was thanks to Orpheus, yet Eurydice alone can do a lot too. She is not a shadow, unfortunately, she is a woman.

What I never understood is how such a beautiful cittern ended up in the hands of the equally beautiful Orpheus. Indeed, it's not clear how they are still together.

Maybe there is a mother watching over them. Maybe she's waiting for the spring to end its song and for Orpheus to go back to his great mysteries.

Yet, Chicca, we still don't know what destiny is.

Doll

The doll that was never born chirps slowly, as if she were a child sacrificed to intelligence.

Yet it is a child in flesh and bone that loves you, my darling, the child within me.

Beauty

A man enters, he's reproaching a girl.

Man: 'Get up, you fool, come and write for me: "I am your Lord".'

Girl: 'And who's decided this?'

Man: 'Your own grace: beautiful girls are meant to serve.'

Girl: 'But I'm a graceful woman.'

Man: 'Precisely because you are graceful you must die: other women do not like you.'

Girl: 'Despite you being an animal, remember I am an animal just like you. Don't be fooled by my beauty, I could become just like you.'

Man: 'If you're like me then our remark will not make any sense. You will stay beautiful despite my abuses. I will throw sand bags at you, so that your internal bleeding won't show. You'll suffer like hell. You'll live in the dream which to you will become delirium. You will seem good from the outside, yet within you will harbour revenge. You will never show signs of tiredness and abuse. Despite being pure, you'll be belittled by everyone.'

Girl: 'Why are you doing this to me?'

Man: 'Because I can be cruel, you know that well, and you need to learn that cruelty too is of God's creation and that I can play with you forever, till death. No one will ever know that evil has visited your depths. No one will ever know the cause of your death. Your face is well suited for theatrical imagination, and I'll make a whining, speechless dog out of you.'

Suddenly a light falls between them. The monster cracks in two and the girl dies of love.

Glasses

At our house, large sets of glasses, used for so many guests, for parties and reconciliations, for births and weddings, lay inside a nice showcase in place of books. My mother would hand one to each guest.

Fresh and clinking, of pure crystal or cheap glass, they would symbolise the wealth of our house, they were a sign of how we lived and of how hospitable we were.

Those crystal sheaths filled with the nectar of friendship were a testimony of our hospitality.

Yet the poor drinks straight form the source, without glasses.

Maybe the most beautiful glass that Nature has to offer is the human hand.

Jewellery

A painful topic. In the eighteenth century, if I remember correctly, to hide certain unpleasant smells ladies would place small sachets under their armpits, in their groin, in all those places chiefly involved in the process of love-making.

Thus, at the key moment, those sachets would gently burst, filling the air with sweet and pleasant perfumes which would invite their lovers to the boldest, most forbidden erotic intimacies.

The fragrance, the perfume, has often taken the place of public decency. The same applies to jewels, and affectation, and all such tools that have brought to light a very primitive and vain side of women: the wish to appear, to show a shrewd image of themselves.

Where there isn't a delicate care, a sober, tasteful simplicity not many can muster, there you have frills. To cover a stain, say, or a foul smell.

Women have always used such arrangements to better appreciate themselves, to trick, to gratify themselves.

Women have always been very inventive in matters of frills and fashion. Ablutions, charms, vices: all stratagems that are meant to distract, like when a necklace gets caught on the lover's watch. Such arrangements are meant to simulate love, to attract men's attention, to give an impression of a progressive, carefree life.

My easy life, instead, only allows me to wear deadlocks and keys around my neck. I've bought all sorts of types, though they only last a day, since I fall asleep on my jewellery like Cleopatra. And in the morning I find myself naked – no trace of trinkets left. Yet way more beautiful than when I had lain in bed.

Dark

The boy I'd like to possess has a cold, childish soul, yet his body is extremely masculine. I would be able to use it, were it not that he keeps telling me about poetry, showing off his ambition. Now I know what it is.

Ambition is the will to make others shiver without reason, choosing oneself as one's own role model, setting one's ego at the centre of one's existence. The ambitious man makes other people shiver because he shivers himself with the lust for power. Then everyone suffers because of this initial mistake.

Whereas, the humble monk seeks the simple grass, that which satisfies him most.

We've never taught our children what joy really is, but we should set up a school of happiness.

Honest people do not know happiness, since while they sleep they do not repeat themselves, do not bleed, do not work, do not occupy the realm of reason; and reason is like an old nest where poets go to sleep.

Driving a poet out in the dead of winter is not easy, since the poet is lazy, so lazy she wants to hide in the dark.

The dark is so painless, so much like a hedge, so much like a mum.

Slander

Slander is a toothless word which, when it reaches its target, wears iron jaws.

Each year a new slander is born, like a fresh egg.

Slander is immodest and maybe it doesn't even have words of itself, it is reasoned and planned at a lonely table at night.

Slander is the result of ignorance or of the lack of something: a dreamt-of affection, a virtue, or the unjustified absence of words form the closest of one's relatives. When stories are repeated mindlessly, words are connected and combined, and thus slander becomes unavoidable.

Slander follows a logic of dramatization and can be used against anyone, even us. After all, the greatest victim of slander is the innocent.

Writers like to slander themselves, find themselves fat, infected, unhealthy and slightly lewd. They refrain from sin only to say that they are not vicious enough for the society, and, because society is vicious where there is no suspicion, the seductive face of slander appears.

Musically, slander does not exist, it's a spoiling of genius and of all its temperamental sides. On the other hand, the genius complains of itself, since it needs slander to live. And it learns to pay the price of its hearings going from one editor to the other.

Camellias

Why do you chase me and step on me day and night and never leave me in peace? I know you're behind me, I can feel your mocking breath on my body.

Your stare skews my path, mixes up my windows, drips like a rivulet of blood inside my vagina.

You have troubled my chastity with your finger, aiming at the only string of my viola. And you've sang of fury and terror.

I'd like to kill you as you have killed me, though if I were to take off that cold mask you wear on your heart, I would see you don't even have muscles; you're not even alive.

You are a ghost, something that has taken the shape of a dark, warty man, histrionic and warlock-like, swollen with sea and sulphurous appetites as I had never seen.

If you are the devil many have damned, why don't you damn yourself?

Do explain, you liar, why I find the same camellias on my face every morning. And why everyone asks about my age and tells me I don't show it. They don't know you undress and confuse me every night.

I'd like to see you hanged from my genealogic tree, because you've offended my old ones, still and bearded people, with only one bridal room to share among all of them.

You are the ghost that no blade could ever kill; in vain, I pray rosaries against your ugliness, hoping you'll rot. Pray that you'll feed off the only worm that has nourished you.

Still, you have a hand on your belly as if to cover the only thing that keeps you going: violence.

Your phallus must be ugly as night, ugly and foolish as your face.

You are as hairy as an ape; you are devilishly smart. You are hunchbacked, disfigured, ruthless.

Yet, despite being a ghost, you are alive, because you don't have a definite name. You are called asylum.

Candelabrum

Enter two male nurses.

First nurse: 'We brought you here by force and you didn't even notice. You were absolutely colourless, slimy like leprosy. Who knows if, dumb as you are, you've ever realised you are a woman. I'd like to know.'

Second nurse: 'Look at her, she looks like a bird, a bird caught in an empty trap. She's skin and bone, bloodless and scared – a young old lady, unable, surely, to give birth, to complain and especially to flee from here.'

First nurse: 'How old are you, you pretty gipsy?'

The girl looks down at the floor. 'You would never count a wanderer's years. You wouldn't believe it, but I was living hanging on to an intense wish for loneliness. It was like a gigantic candelabrum, and there were many lights, in a big, festive palace. I was, it seemed to me, the Cinderella of the universe. You're looking for my shoes, I can see, but I've lost them in the midst of my long path.

'I love you too, you know? Are you servants of a great prince or king?'

First nurse: 'This one here thinks herself a princess.'

The girl stares at him: 'Haven't you realised, you talking like that, that you're the master of the universe? Have you never thought that the whole sky is yours, the earth is yours, that you can go where you wish, that you are healthy and free from evil?'

First nurse: 'Me, free from evil?'

'Yes, it is evil that makes us small. It is evil that makes you believe that I'm walking barefoot and that in the past I have not been just the same as Joan of Arc.'

Second nurse: 'And what did you want to conquer, say, you poor fool?'

Girl: 'The world!'

Second nurse: 'And what about now that you're in here?'

Girl: 'I don't know where I am. I only know that this is a place, and it's a place where anything can happen, as within your mind. The mind, old watchman, is no different than a place, or the world.'

First nurse: 'Maybe she's right...'

Second nurse: 'Oh, come on! If we were to give credit to anyone who's sectioned here, we'd lose our own minds too.'

First nurse: 'Yet, she still has her beauty, mark of the divine.'

Second nurse: 'The devil was beautiful too, she could be the daughter of a devil. After all, if she thinks sleeping on the grass or between these walls is the same, we could kill her.'

The girl looks up: 'Killing me would only be a matter of tiredness. I arrived here exhausted, so even death would mean some rest, but then so would communication. In truth you don't want to hurt anyone, since you are yourselves already hurt to death.'

Second nurse, slapping her: 'You have no right to judge us.'

The girl pulls herself together: 'It feels like you've taken me to court, but then we are all before the court – I know well that your weapon is contradiction and that you will send me to the stake like Joan of Arc. Yet I've lived through my elementary war and I feel like a lost word.

'In here years fall without meaning, and it's as if the manna were being eaten by pigs.'

'You don't even open your mouth to feed off the freshness of the soul, you don't know the opulence of the sun, you don't know the scent of your own feet, and the impulse of deep pleasure that life causes.

'Tell me, have you ever been children?'

First nurse: 'Yes, two proper rascals.'

Girl: 'I haven't. Let me tell you, at ten I was already an adult and I knew all the words necessary to put a poem together. Poems, you know, are of the same dimensions as the sea.

'But if you turn words upside down you can find the danger of a lie and I know that all the liars are led in here.'

First nurse: 'We don't have chains for liars.'

Girl: 'Yet you put a limit to their space. Just think that a nail can symbolise silence and that a straw bed can deny forever the softness of pain.'

First nurse: 'Is there pain in life?'

Girl: 'Of course! Pain is like blood, it creaks inside the walls and it can even move them. It could knock down this old hospital.'

Second nurse: 'What an idiotic thing to say!'

Girl: 'The hands that have torn off the grass, that have hit to death a sign of life, can even squash my face. You could step on me, but I would only turn into freshly mashed grapes: the recesses of dreams don't live nor die. I feel confused because, sadly, I am horribly happy. So happy I'll let myself fall into your hands.'

Flesh

Today I say goodbye to a friend, a poet and a teacher. A teacher of silence and of humble comfort. His age doesn't say anything, but then neither does mine.

For a long time I wished to change my life and I did, thanks to a young lover. I rolled inside his soul like a ball of wool. The cat saw me, and he was bothered by its strange anomaly.

I was explaining earlier today that a poet becomes a genius when he falls in love. A universal spark, so alike maternal love, ignites inside his heart.

Today I also wrote to my love that I never want to see him again.

He fooled me. He told me, in all his candour, that he has never really desired me, that for him the flesh doesn't exist yet.

Though a fortune teller told me he's got to be smarter than the devil, because in twenty-six years you're bound to feel the flesh.

Still I would have to raise some questions. Could it not be that the flesh of a boy is poetry already? Or is it that my spirit is not fit to understand his carnality? This is a quandary that torments all lovers and philosophers.

Yet I think this young boy has indeed given me something: the soul.

He came with his thoughtlessness and lit this big pile of wood still wet with tears. A fire broke out. The miracle happened once again.

Clinical Folder

Lietta Manganelli[3] calls me with a rosy, distracted voice. Now she is not distrustful as she was when she was a child and, seeing me, she would hold onto her mum's skirt – she had gathered I was a dangerous rival.

I ask her for my old memories, she asks me for my new ones. On this melody of disappointments eternal justice is established.

She and I were lovers of a single great destiny.

Yet Lietta is now worried once more, worried she'll discover I am still the old infanticide, the one who virtually abandoned her. From the ashes of this fear a paper love has risen.

The dream travels through me like a shiver; I open my legs thinking that the moon hangs over one world only, that of restorations.

Workmen have been demolishing my house for a long time and I read a secret joke between the lines of this horror and racket.

Manganelli[4] had entered in here and had sat staring piously at the ceiling. It was a hemispherical ceiling with a portrait of a dead man at its top.

Giorgio had started with: 'Have pity on my long tales and my endless rhymes.'

I had straightened his tie and I had told him that it isn't so sad after all to have your shoes always untied. In return, he had advised me to cover my breasts as I was showing too much cleavage. Manganelli, a nobleman, looked at his common girl, very young back then, like Jerusalem would look at the wrong Solomon.

---

[3] Daughter of Giorgio Manganelli (see footnote n. 4) [TN].

[4] Italian journalist, avant-garde writer, translator and literary critic [TN].

We had learnt together that horror is to share, like love, and we had happily gotten into a swamp of fools who would sleep on our legs; many little Lilliputians who wanted to blow their words into our mouths at all costs.

The dwarfs, with their minuscule ropes, had nailed us to the floor; Manganelli used to say laughingly: 'We'll get rid of them sooner or later.' But it isn't easy to get rid of dwarfs, as it isn't easy to get rid of workmen.

Edgar Allan Poe's crooked smile looks at me from behind the falling window. I think of the house of Ushers and I see the flaking off of a gigantic cotton wool underneath my only light blue gown.

Confused hallucinations have hit me in the heart, so I start to write a silly thing that goes like this: 'I am a little fossil shell with an engine malfunction.'

Yet Manganelli is shaking now, he goes up and down the stairs shouting at the workmen to leave, screaming: 'Sleeping Beauty lives here, shabby looking but very quick at calculations. By now, this woman who is a crater of shame will never resuscitate, but no one shall violate her sight.'

Manganelli's tie flutters slightly while he tells me that recently Lacan has found a new folder in the memory, an additional one to those stored by Sigmund Freud. Might he be referring to my forlorn clinical folder, lost inside a bouquet of roses?

Meanwhile, Sleeping Beauty still thinks she's left, on a day like any other, going out of the same window from where Kant's ghost used to come in, when he was tired of scaring people.

She recognised in M.'s dull face her Matriarch Syndrome. She, the bony psychiatrist, has just thrown someone out the window to get rid of them and speak once more of destiny's courses and recourses.

Apparently Prozac is not good for you and whoever takes it has authoritative suicidal impulses; strange impulses going from vacuous to serene. Yet death, alas, is no more than a hanger bought at the Naviglio market[5].

I'm not sure, but there seems to be an inexplicable relationship between the death of a woman who has miserably vanished and this foreboding witch breathing over my shoulders; this young, toothless Berenice, who is me, who is her, doubly fused in a single horror of memories. We love each other desperately.

His tender loins are very jealous of my skin; at night his hands empty my vagina of the many eggs I have brooded in silence. I feel my veins slipping out one by one with the initial rush of pleasure and I fall into an orgasm caused by the electroshock.

My jaws open, I shout frantically at the climax of pleasure while he kisses me, right here, on the back of my neck, where I die of love. And while he kisses me, his eyes go to the clock.

Midnight tolls and Cinderella is finally lost.

---

[5] Famous market in Milan [TN].

Postcards

A friend of mine has a full collection of postcards that soldiers would send from the front during the war.

Neat, studied calligraphies, fiery kisses and hot ladies.

Soldiers kept those love fetishes underneath their pillows, while women, desired and repudiated because of the war, waited for their lovers, hoping prayers could save their lives.

Soldiers: those kind-hearted boys who reluctantly went to defend their homeland, who left their family and risked to die – they were all in love.

All those living at the edge of death fall in love. Because love too, as death, is scary. Thus, not knowing what to fear anymore, one entity accompanies the other, one entity exorcises the other. Yet love is the most beautiful euthanasia there is.

Drawer

Michele Pierri[6] told me he was hopelessly bad at medicine, and in fact he had been a doctor all his life. More specifically, he could not stand the sight of blood.

It was the blessed Moscati[7] who vehemently pushed him into the operating room. The blessed had no mercy on the poor man who, forced into a skimpy jacket, did not know how nor did he want to operate. Thus Moscati made him into a valuable surgeon.

After all, a poet is great not only on one side, he is great all round. He is something else.

Thus Michele Pierri would seek rest from the sight of blood in his poetry, wonderful for that matter, which has sadly been forgotten. No one took care of spreading his writings, which he had kept shamefully stored away in a drawer.

Maybe the blessed Moscati had explained to Michele Pierri that poetry was a sin to be hidden, because it distracted him.

It is true, poetry is a potent distraction from pain, from the heavy things in life. Poetry is also a chain, though a chain made of flowers.

Today there's only me left to remember Michele Pierri, along with his ardent poems that touch my heart.

---

[6] Italian poet and doctor from Taranto and husband of Alda Merini from 1984 [TN].

[7] Famous Italian doctor [TN].

Blowpipe

Why do people sometimes block the path of those going their own way searching for a soul and seeking risk for their family? For years, I've had the same troubles as you. However, strangely, though looking for the meaning of existence at home, I never found it.

Now that you've reached the door of silence, I'd like to know how you're finding it, because I've talked so much in order to make you understand that I love you. Who knows why writers put together entire books to tell a friend or a lover that they care about them.

Yet a brother is so much more, he has the same blood as you, the same rage, the same stubbornness. You both are neither too fragile, neither too beautiful.

The two of us were rams used to overcoming obstacles. We never cried together, we both have a strong nature.

To keep me calm you would tell me strange lies, for instance that the Three Wise Men would not come for Christmas. You always had fun playing pranks on me, like when you were little and you would sneakily get your blowpipes ready to aim at my eyes. I've always fallen for your tricks.

Yet, beware, I'm not falling for this one. Your death really is an impossible trick.

Key

I lost a key once. I had attempted to build it throughout the years, trying to smooth it out, to gild it nicely and, lastly, to find a keyhole for it.

Nonetheless, despite there being many doors in the neighbourhood, none of them fit my key, because each key wants a hole and each hole wants its silence.

Since I was so desperate in my search for the hole, some good-natured and mischievous neighbours hanged the key at my neck. With that cowbell hanging there, looking like a baby, I wandered incredulous, thinking sadly that I did not have a home.

To dwell means to stop, and to stop means to bless, and to bless means to wait. Hence that key was the start of a great chance. No one knew that, having been manipulated by many, it had ended up in the hands of a wizard.

This was a boorish and chubby wizard who would shoot fiery blows at fortune in order to change the course of the stars, yet he hadn't taken into account that philosophy is stronger than the reasons of the zodiac. That is why I wouldn't find the door nor, equally obstinately, could I lose the key.

One day the wizard sent a kid to tell me to leave the neighbourhood because the cursed key had infected the whole area. But I could not leave that place, because that was a God-fearing key.

Until a lousy thief came running and ripped it off my neck.

I stood there stunned, looking at the road with my naked throat, without key, without luck.

Then I thought that, after all, each sky has not one but a thousand doors, so I tried opening at least one of those who do not need keys, but Saint Peter rejected me too.

Eventually I had a blacksmith making me a new one, very flashy, and everyone was afraid of it.

Since then rumour has it that with that key I open the mysterious doors of many destinies.

Cinema

I have been a cinema enthusiast, I have loved many films. I have learnt history through epic movies.

Now I don't go to the cinema anymore, the last film I watched was *Léon*. A very intense, painful film: a little girl and a killer have to undergo terrible ordeals.

The feeling of revenge dripped from those two bodies like black pitch. Both full of love, they were looking for justice, which they had already forgiven. More importantly, they feared injustice.

I have often asked myself whether in love injustice should be forgiven or not.

Corriere della Sera[8]

There is a street in Milan which leads to the *Corriere della Sera*, where Ranieri[9] sits at his desk. That of the newspaper headquarters is a stern building, and very stern was Montale[10] too, when he worked there.

Eugenio weighed me with a look of comparison from his desk the first time he saw me; he could tell I would be a not so loyal contestant.

In those times of joyful follies of my first youth I was coming fresh out of Quasimodo[11]'s bed, and Montale began to hate me quite serenely. It was the wonderful Maria Luisa[12] who stood up for me.

I adored Maria Luisa Spaziani, a great teacher for me, but also a brave companion. Great poets don't fall into greed; they're kind-hearted, they can devote themselves beyond love's cowardice.

After Manganelli's death, Ebe Flamini[13] thanked me for my discretion, though after all I couldn't have done with his cultural heritage what Spaziani did so generously with Montale's. I didn't have the space, nor the ability, nor the professionalism. Nor the memories. In ten years of hospitalisation I had lost sight of Giorgio. And despite the fact that, once I had come out of the asylum, he had started again to recount to me what had happened, I just could not reach him anymore.

The day Manganelli died, Ranieri sent for me.

---

[8] Famous Italian newspaper [TN].

[9] Ranieri Polese, journalist for the *Corriere della Sera* [TN].

[10] Eugenio Montale, famous Italian poet of the 20th century [TN].

[11] Salvatore Quasimodo, famous Italian poet of the 20th century [TN].

[12] Maria Luisa Spaziani, famous Italian poet of the 20th century [TN].

[13] Partner of Giorgio Manganelli [TN].

For months he had left a sealed envelope with five thousand liras for me at the *Corriere*, without ever coming to me. I was hungry at the time, yet instead of buying food I would waste money around, while Polese would laugh and would keep leaving his scarlet letters at the reception. Yet when Manganelli died I closed the chapter of Via Solferino[14].

That day Ranieri told me, looking me in the eyes sternly, that I should have confronted the critics to get something of Giorgio's. The most beautiful and surprising thing, however, I got from his daughter: a big photo of Manganelli wearing a robe. Thus I learnt that my spiritual tutor had graduated in canonical and civil law. I found out he had taken a path that went in the opposite direction to literature.

---

[14] The road that hosted the newspaper headquarters [TN].

Kitchen

My kitchen hasn't been hot for years; no one eats in it anymore. I feed myself sandwiches, sprawled on the bed, looking at walls that are to be erased.

I couldn't dine in the kitchen without my husband and children.

If it gets late I sometimes dine in small restaurants, but it makes little difference. When I get back home there's no boiling pot around.

People often invite me for lunch, but I almost never accept. It would feel like drinking tea in the desert, like having no one around the table.

Anyway, because it feels like I'm not fulfilling a duty, I send food to the poor, so that they can feed secretly, like I do.

Lately I've been thinking that food, which is so fundamental for many, can become a poison.

I told my daughter that I've received many invites for Easter, yet the truth is I want to be on my own. I cannot look a family in the face anymore, because I'm so ashamed I have grown so distant from mine. Back then my husband would cook. He would make fake, dubious food that no one would eat; he would cook wrong even fried eggs. Yet we would laugh, we would sing. The kids and the guests would eat for two, and there would be no nervous people around.

Nowadays I don't even go and eat at my children's. Once, for Christmas, I had gone to Emanuela. There was a long table laden with food. I asked my daughter what had happened to a poor lady she used to help out who would always eat alone, barefoot, sitting on the sidewalk. A poor madwoman many would say, a poor creature I say. She answered that the woman had died for the cold. So I got up, went back to my house and filled my mouth with pure bread.

After all, my husband too, every Christmas, would invite a poor to our table and it made us so happy to see those eyes reddened from the cold, staring at us with infinite tenderness. Our house was very warm back then, and there was soup for everyone.

Our daughters, even when already married, would often come and live with us for a while. They don't anymore now. And when they do come, they only speak of their dad with me, and I too, after all, only speak of him with them.

Yet there's one thing my kids haven't understood: his death hasn't saddened me, I am happy, because he is still inside here, that's why I cannot forget him. We should not cry for the dead, we should only hope for them.

Crimes

The pleasure your body gives me, beyond any obscure opinion, is not comparable to any song, and no poem could ever sing of you. Because nothing lives ahead of you, I could never utter a single word, so great is the astonishment that leads me to the altar of your wedding.

Love poems pour out of the shame of having been born before you and of having touched, clad in casualty, your young body.

You do not know me; you could never compare yourself to the many crimes of my life and to the many pressing sorrows. Yet why have people and culture spoken of sorrow instead of colour?

Once I saw a man who, in the grip of his violence, tried to kill me; he came on top of me like a hawk and I pitifully let my neck be lowered by his arm. Then he disappeared, swallowed by the darkness.

In that moment I saw Cain attacking Abel, guilty of owning bigger pearls and moans. In that moment I saw God's approval. And I understood that that man was my true brother, him whom I loved right after God himself.

I understood this when his hand retracted and he was so generous with his crime.

Kinder than my chastity.

Devil

I have often asked myself if it is worth to sell your soul to the devil in order to have a life full of lies, but at least a loyal existence, honest in the eyes of everyone.

Lucifer was the torch of Paradise.

My God, how I could change: entering darkness, taking it in my hands and feeing off it as if it were manna.

Breathe with painted nostrils, as those of a clown, the silence of poetry and especially the silence of pain.

And to think that each human being is an earthquake on earth, a war ready to break out any minute.

The devil, that secret friend of mine who gives me his hand when I sigh for you, who pushes me to silence my guilt and who leads my steps towards your hidden ways.

I have never confessed to you my sweet secrets, that I am your coward and your honey.

Look, while you are not here I invoke my enemy and you don't even notice you've gotten inside his mourning clothes.

I am a possessed woman, I know, but more than that I am a man trying to contain a woman; and you in turn become a miserable, hellish song.

Cursed hedges and distracted settlers built this meadow of love where the devil runs and races with his hard, destructive speech.

Yet, if you think about it well enough, you can't call yourself a man if you don't think a bit about the texture of his mind.

It is there, where sin generated its flower, that the man becomes a cheater by nature, a barycentre of horror. What we call love is nothing other than the devil's mockery.

The devil dismays us, seduces us, he is eternally drunk on our presence. In such incessant state of intoxication he inhabits the islands of the senses, where young virgins turn their grace into dance.

That is where the thread tangles and the parasite of fear makes us feel its endless dismay.

Yet now the time has come to think about how easy it is to descend the hill of reason to foolishly give oneself to sin. Because sin is not that unhealthy numbness everyone believes. Passion is not that magic circle which can tear the root of our eyes.

Sin, Guido, is remaining flawed near a front door, near a little threshold left ajar which will never truly open because the devil is blind. And like all poets he cannot distinguish between the air and a sip of water.

Dilemma

This sad lord of doubt has charmed the public with a speech that has no logic, no harmony, no internal happiness.

Hamlet has no doubts, he is sure, but as the man of thought he is, a coward like all poets, he wants people to believe he is unsure. He confuses the enemies, surprises them, meanwhile he hides in indignation.

Yet what is Hamlet's madness if not a great Oedipal complex which pushes him to ignore himself? Hamlet uses a ghost to give a face to his face, to that anxiety that leads him to persecute his only love, to barge into the scene like a rabid dog who does not feel true hunger.

Hamlet is not a slave to a hostile destiny; if he had kept quiet and faked ignorance he would have avoided his fate. Yet he wants to fight against the ghosts of his mind. He is not fighting against his mother, nor against his step-father, nor against his madness, which has proved itself to be extremely right.

Hamlet fights against his demons, and these images, these revenges, are not against others but against what troubles him. Anxiety or celestial language? Going to meet his own breath on the stage, what is Hamlet looking for if not his vanity, his glory and his dishonour? And is it actually true that glory brings dishonour and that dishonour is glory?

It can happen, sometimes, that such contradiction may triumph so highly as to wipe out others' intelligence. So highly as to become theatre. Yet can a genius wipe out the revenges of the actions solely by himself? Hamlet knows he cannot. Which is why he chooses to kill: he has no other solution.

Mess

There is order in my house, but no one sees it. Everyone sees an enthralling mess, but dare not say so because they feel bad.

After all, with my mess I have healed many neuroses. Whoever resists in my house for at least two hours is already on their way to healing. Everyone leaves shocked but happy; they finally revalue the clean streets, the over-polished bars, the fresh restaurants and the formalities of romantic dinners.

In my house you can never kiss – between me and my lover there's always a big Easter *colomba*[15] or a dessert spilt on the table dividing us.

My daughter says I am messy because I'm afraid to love. I think she is right.

---

[15] An Italian Easter cake in the shape of a dove [TN].

Distances

The informal appellative[16] does not allow replies, the formal one instead creates space for discussion. With the informal appellative you can start a subtle violence; it's almost like initiating love-making. Addressing someone formally is essential towards having the right sense of balance.

We kids used the formal appellative to address our father, thus establishing the right distance between the parent and the child in the hierarchy of souls. Such formality was not sheer discipline, it meant that he had generated us not through sex but with his mind, his audacity.

He guided our will with his mind, he was the educator. The quintessential good and just man.

The informal 'you' was a loving flower that mother and father exchange, not children, thus the latter respected the former.

A certain type of winking, or patting under the table, coming from our father or mother would mean they were not angry at us anymore, that they had forgiven us that distant formal 'you'.

---

[16] In Italian the pronoun 'you' is distinguished between a singular form '*tu*' and plural form '*voi*'; the plural form '*voi*' is used to refer to a single individual as a form of respect [TN].

Enigma

I don't know who you are to overpower me with such shame. I would like to call you by your name, because I love you. But I've never seen your face and I don't know the hairs on your legs. I think you approach me at night like a bear, and you venture beyond my untameable lashes and you want to reflect them in your own face. Because you look at me with icy eyes, the blue eyes of convenience, of roughness and of love. You are white because you wander with the best of swans.

I would like to tell the others I met you when you were still in your prime, something to save and take far.

You solitary deity, who washes and squeezes me, who glorifies and condemns me, who wishes for my blindness and greediness; you deity covered in deceit; you evergreen man, who expelled me thousands of times; you man I do not know, but of whom, directly, I am the daughter.

I would like to ask your left hand what has happened to your will. I am nothing for you, I know. You have deflowered me endless times, without ever asking my name. You have put fiery rods in my chest and then you have made me feign I don't know how many killings.

I am for you like a big Saint Bernard wandering in snow. I try to breath air in you, to make sure you won't fall dead, oh poet, new-born and small, callow as a little girl.

Will you jump the big ditch of laughter alien to all poets? Will you ever know the enigma of your heart?

I want to teach you something. Everyone has within themselves an enigma that no one will ever unravel, a private riddle they will carry around till the end. What do the others cry after all at the time of our death? Not having been able to understand someone who has left together with their mystery.

I would like you, young poet so translucent that everyone recognises you, not to create this enigma, I wish you could continue to fly over the Alp of your possibilities.

If you were to become my lover, you would know my mystery and this would damn you forever. Oh young poet, do not believe the mysteries of the dead. Narcissus, because of a too intense abandonment, fell in love with himself.

Failure

They did not listen to her, Amelia Rosselli[17], the great and divine Amelia, the exquisite poet. No one had time for her, no one could understand her. Psychiatrists were simply satisfied with giving a name to her fear. Yet who has people 'above suspicion' next to them, as I do, knows they have the sacrosanct right to harbour their fears.

The sinner can be happy as a lover, because who cannot do wrong in front of God also can't feel the joy of asking for forgiveness. God loves our failures, he looks at them with a benevolent eye.

And I cry on Amelia's demise, who went away without wanting to give meaning to her death. Yet hers was not a tragic ending, it was not without meaning. When one can't bear life anymore, one wants to die in the arms of God.

---

[17] Famous Italian poet of the 20th century [TN].

Ghosts

The deputy manager of my building is perpetually on holiday; when he goes away he leaves his glass eye to the most reliable neighbour, so that they can update him on everything that went on during his absence.

He's a little bit like the Little butter Man in Pinocchio. He pities me when he sees me alone and says to me: 'Why don't you take in a handyman? He could help you with the household chores. As well as with other "jobs".'

At which point I explain to the deputy that these other jobs I have had performed by respectful people, and to honour these great people I cannot hire just any person, I can hardly receive Ernesto. It's not a question of sex, but rather of mentality and of mind.

Also, my loneliness is an entire population of friends, of ghosts.

The deputy manager does not consider that I am not lacking love. I still do it with Manganelli, with Quasimodo. But how could he know this, he does not believe in ghosts.

Fairy-tales

It's night. Women begin to have a time of forgiveness.

I rest in front of a video which is finally free, which doesn't speak anymore of the things that ruin people's mind.

I am watching a cartoon with great natural festivities, with fairy-tales and punishment for the baddies. That's how life should be, that's how I wish it would be.

The prince kisses his Snow White and I see myself dumbfounded in the arms of a handsome young man. How sweet is his kiss and how assertive is Snow White when she catches his lips. She is not a girl, she is a woman. And the prince blushes at the revelation of her maturity.

Dear me, the great cartoons of our childhood, the great cartoons that we are. Why does the modern man have to think of fairy-tales to create himself anew?

Why do we need to become children again to live?

When I was little, my mother used to tell me about Pandora releasing her winds. Now and then, at night, Pandora with her white shirt still comes to me and terrorises me, at the age of sixty.

It's night. I look at myself in the mirror and I untie my hair, which becomes wonderfully long and white.

Finally the fear of life shows itself; the whiteness of old age drives its way through the darkness of the swamp. I see in the mirror that I have been insulted and offended for many years and behind me I can feel the sneer of a snake-like man, that I identify as the idiot.

Oh yes, the idiot. The genius also knows how to be stupid and as such they end up in an asylum.

I have become horrible. It's ten o'clock at night and I look like a witch. My face is covered in wrinkles, scarlet with rage. I am not different from the evil witch in Snow White.

I too would like to kiss a prince. My lips are dry, I miss nature's kisses, I miss air's kiss and I see that the mirror is crying. It seems to me it is swinging from wall to wall, as if I could be the one to free it from that white bug that time is.

I saw hell once. Tiny devils were jumping on my hands with an incredible fork which took away my fingertips. They would fall like petals of unfair roses, they had quite a wretched smell and from pink they would turn into black lying petals, petals of a too bitter path.

Have I been happy? I would say always and never. Always happy when I had ebony-black hair, always desperate when my hair would fall and I would turn into the Bald Singer or the Little Match Girl. I believed editors were gigantic sulphur matches who were there to warm up a cold street.

Now there aren't any Lilliputians anymore, only giants, and the poor Gulliver is yet to be found; like Alice he's become tiny and maybe too dumb. He's falling.

The Mad Hatter keeps celebrating his unbirthday, yet on the tenth of January I did not receive a single flower. Instead, to make up for it, death came to see me.

I would never have expected her. She tried to smile, but she was repulsive. I welcomed her, since we cannot do without her anyway.

She's a woman, or a monster, who appears at inhospitable hours, when everything seems peaceful.

There, now I'm watching Fantozzi[18]. God forbid that, seeing me so peaceful, she appears again.

---

[18] Ugo Fantozzi, fictional character created by famous Italian comedian Paolo Villaggio [TN].

Foil

I've fallen in love with a young man pure as light who has promised me death.

Do not think that I'm harbouring wicked thoughts, only some private considerations. Promising death gives a sense of clearness, or rather of clarity. Instead, promising a gift, even if from one's own body, means tricking life.

He has promised me death because I haven't asked him anything, nor the head of a rose, nor a hand on my knees, not even an inappropriate visit. However, I have asked him silence. And if it is hard for a young man to keep quiet, imagine for an old man.

The young man is never talkative, yet he speaks volumes. The old man, instead, rambles on and can express himself only when he's leaning on a cane.

I remember once an old man came to see me. With his cane he pointed at my hard-earned papers and told me: 'Give up poetry and the chains of imagination. Maybe you will manage to live.'

Everyone thinks imagination is a free act. Yet that's not true, you always come back to the great hunger of the earth, to the great nuisance of our lives.

Yes, you can unsheathe imagination, like a wonderful foil pointing at the mask of protection the lover is always wearing.

Few know I am the granddaughter of a fencing champion and that I have spent the happiest hours of my life on the stands during the Olympics. And because nature hasn't given me a body too swift, she nonetheless gave me a certain mental agility, so that I learnt to fence with the eyes.

Bad fencer is the lover and bad springboard am I. Yet both duellists wear a pre-established mask. Love is always a fencing tournament, it's always a duel to the death.

It's hard to establish during these competitions who the real enemy is. What is essential though is greet each other at the start of every match. The person who gets 'touched' is the one who, nobly, apologises to the other.

And the whole thing will resolve with the deposition of the weapon in front of the clapping public.

Flowers

Back in the days I too have studied the Ikebana. The composition of flowers, the goal of flowers, the animistic meaning of flowers, the letters of flowers. And I have also received many flowers, yet, to tell you the truth, I have never understood them.

The other day, for instance, an admirer sent me a bouquet of camellias, but I chose to exchange them for carnations.

Yes, of course, the camellia is beautiful, fragrant, yet it looks like a small cabbage. Actually, on second thought, it doesn't smell nice at all, which is synonym of a cold woman.

Poor Traviata[19], who tricked her lover into believing she did not love him, who went dancing here and there saying she had no time to lose. Poor Traviata. How happy she would have been to sleep on these thornless camellias.

---

[19] The protagonist of Verdi's opera based on Dumas's *Lady of the Camellias* [TN].

Leaves

Leaves have the exact outline of our beauty when they blossom once more into graceful ornaments. They are scattered perpendiculars, they are needles of shiver, of fear.

Our language does not have a single dialect, and yet during spring days it becomes irregular and meaningless, because it shakes with leaves.

I brought a bouquet of useless roses to a useless boy, I did it because I wanted to probe my past ground: they were the same roses I had picked from the ground of my madness and which I was giving back to him now.

Time's duration inside the mind of the poet who writes has the sobriety of a blossoming flower. Poetry, too, is a rainfall of petals; poetry, too, swallows tears and resolves itself.

There are images madness feeds on as if they were magnolias, images which will never reoccur.

Poetry is a great eater of eroticism, she is a great carnivorous. She has devoured your face too and will devour many more.

She does this because she is hungry and thirsty of leaves. She does this because she is hungry and thirsty of people.

To feed poetry you don't need to be better or worse, you just need to let yourself live thinking that every mirror could be the last, that every day could be the last.

At this point, I contain within me all the germs of my narrative, yet not because I have been born on the first day of spring, but rather because, by the grace of God, I renew myself every morning, and will do so until summer will make me fall down.

It will be then that, without any desire left for men or women, I will become a perfect fruit for God's unilateral mind.

Photographs

The photograph, be it refined or of high regard, be it votive or be it a snap-shot, it is always a fruit of art. The photographer has to handle the most humble things and turn them into masterpieces. There are people who are photogenic and those who aren't, there are people who adhere to the lens and those who drive it away because magnetism is not reflected in the camera.

My brother is an agile photographer, he was the one who portrayed me young for the first time, he was the one to establish certain distances, certain lights which I then learnt by heart.

I was his favourite model. Yet today he does not take pictures anymore, he's too busy thinking of medicines' dosages. He's become a far-away man who will never repeat himself.

It's incredible how doctors can melt people like mints in water to make a tisane, a mush, an elderly thing out of them, all of a sudden. You become old when you start taking note of your delusions and of the times when you need to take your medication.

I was like that too, but then I managed to get rid of that. My brother, however, does not believe in me anymore, he believes only in his doctors: I have lost him. I have lost a peculiar man, a person of great morals, who had always opposed medical intervention. Now I know he wants to go.

Maybe he hasn't said everything to me, maybe he didn't want to let me know that silence was betraying us. We both understood this, and that's why we haven't been talking to each other for two months.

Legs

Legs in a woman are the enhancement of her will.

The erotic leg lazily abandoned on the bed is a natural solicitation for unrest.

As soon as the man will touch that lifeless limb he will become an agile runner, he will bend over backwards to provide blood and peace to those irreplaceable shapes, perfect both for idleness and for procreation.

Yet the legs of a woman have many eyes a man does not see and many lips he does not notice. They are eyes and lips looking for love, yes, but also for the life of love.

Jealousy

You are the sweetest of birches, full of movement, not yet interdicted by divine justice.

God still hasn't taken into account your infinite grace, otherwise he would have already punished you.

He is so jealous of his own beauty that he could not remain indifferent in front of you.

Jewels

I find that gold does not suit me. I have always been full of superstitions. I believe that the horn[20] drives the devil away, that the chain intrigues the lover and that a pearl necklace gives me the semblance of a great lady.

On the other hand, I have always been an eager reader of the Bible too, I have copied bits here and there about the Queen of Sheba and I have learnt how to be a Jerusalem.

Indeed, tonight a lady asked me: 'Since you are so famous, how come you don't have a place entitled to you?' In truth I do have one. At least until someone displaces me.

Meanwhile you can call me Jerusalem delivered[21].

---

[20] Horn-shaped pendant, commonly used lucky charm in Italy [TN].

[21] Reference to the epic poem of the same name by the Italian poet Torquato Tasso [TN].

Fool

I get up and arrange three carrots on the floor. Here in the asylum you cannot cook, but I'm thinking today of setting up a school and I know carrots are good for your eyesight. My students will all be soothsayers.

Yet there has been a time when, if I'm not mistaken, I have been a mother.

There is a fool outside my window that goes to and fro all day and all night. I would like to ask him if a woman, or better a mother, can become a child.

The fool has the sweetest look in his eyes and seems to be blond. Yet how come is Guido freely wandering around asylums? And how do I know his name?

If I were to call him and he would answer, I would be scared to death. Because it would mean that I am a fairy or an old soul.

Yet he is not a doctor, nor a physician, nor an affected intellectual. He lives in a castle that is all of his own, yet he does not care about me. Maybe he doesn't even know I live in his manor and that the wing hosting me is called 'asylum'.

Why is he a free man and I a prisoner? Why is the lord to whom I have attributed so many courtiers always alone? Why doesn't he ever sit down? Why doesn't he cry?

I am fond of this young man, because I too never cry. He doesn't know, alas, that his thoughts are guided by me, that I am the one who governs him.

And yet I have never thought, nor dreamt of him coming to rescue me, because he is fine without me and I am fine behind those bars.

Deceit

Let's talk about Othello's jealousy and of his spiritual unworthiness. Othello is a magnate of faults, a magnanimous of faults, a man who feels deceived by his own colour. A man who sees in Desdemona's sweetness an offense to his misery. A man who feels hated and who despite everything has risen to glory.

It isn't Iago who betrays Othello, it is Othello who awaits the confirmation of his suspicion; it is Othello who is waiting for the chance to die for love, to turn a great passion into ashes.

Every poet and prophet knows how the end of their life is going to happen, and they seek it desperately so that the only truth, love, won't slip away from their hands. Only with the lamp of love you see things that appear dark under the light.

Othello, who feels deceived by his fear, is instead looking for allies to confuse him.

I am a poet who has never seen Venice, who does not know what the fury of water is.

Yet maybe I am a poet precisely because of this: because in my poverty I had to imagine everything and I did it so well that it's like I have been eternally travelling.

There are words which have riled up my fantasy to the point where I imagined seeing things I have never seen. They often invite me, but I don't want to travel to visit other lands anymore; they have been denied to me when I was young.

Yet I have travelled a lot through the men that have loved me, with them I have read the whole Elizabethan theatre. Maybe you don't need a vast culture to write, maybe you only need to obey your fate to write. Maybe I wouldn't even have stood Venice.

So I reject you, my love, because to love you I just need my imagination.

Anger

Anger is the most extraordinary event that can happen to a person, and lucky me that I don't hide it. Anger is a vice, it's a mortal sin and the law rightfully keeps it in check. Yet throwing a plate on the floor or swearing repeatedly in poetry is one of the greatest pleasures in life. Cecco Angiolieri[22] wouldn't have existed if he hadn't been angry, sickening, full of bad words, yet always full of words.

Anger causes swearing too, but it's just temporary turmoil that only has the duration of a lightening of words.

I remember being angry, like I am now, already when I was a child. But if I weren't so angry maybe I wouldn't be able to write as much.

My Muses can get on my nerves.

---

[22] A medieval Italian poet, contemporary of Dante Alighieri [TN].

Inspiration

Usually freelancers of thought look for inspiration in different ways: there's the one who sits at the table, the one who sits in front of a blank page, the one who puts on a very serious face and who waits for God to reward them with an unpublished work.

I have chosen the more manual way: I wake up in a bad mood, with a drowsy mouth, and, with my successes forgotten, I complain about the low income coming from the published works and I start swearing.

I don't know why but when I have to write I become violent, I make calls here and there, I hire inexistent killers and decide that I will have justice within the day.

Recently they told me guardian angels are back in fashion, and I must have mine too, because now and then a celestial peace invades me, my head empties completely and I start writing. I don't even need the pen, I just call one of the twenty-four secretaries of the heart and I dictate to them this state of grace.

They themselves don't understand a thing as well, only that I have stolen their time. Yet to my editors, to whom I always complain, I will never tell what I feel when I receive the visit of the inspiration.

Thief

'As long as no one sees me, I steal. No one would guess that that card I hide in a corner, that stolen love letter, that shame about the road taken with skilful deception isn't just a "thing": it is a woman whose imagination has been taken away from me.

Once, in jail, they called me misfit, outcast, extinguished ember; instead I am a great oven that burns flowers. I am a thief.

I live in a hovel, it's true, but at night I put my good rod on the stove and I think. I think the prostitute who lives with me is not a great lady, but she is home.

I love eluding envy; no one can know how great it is to be a thief. Maybe only poets can imagine it. When they write, they must feel the same thrill that I feel when I steal.

The police can shed light on my body as much as they want; the crime is always a safe room. I even have some very fine batiste handkerchiefs, vague female perfumes, stepped-on nails, and a stick with a pointy end: I needed it to gather cigarette studs around the neighbourhood, which I would then unroll and I would make my own cigarette.

People don't know that the thief has the delicate task of keeping the world in balance. Some people have too many pearls and spells on them; they need someone to steal those things from them, and take them away to adorn a naked neck, to fill an empty hand.

The intention of the thief would be to give them to the poor, but he is the first poor, so he is the first rightful beneficiary. Thus the thief mocks himself and regrets having repented so many times; he never feels the need to go to church. For long days he has tasted the hate of people in prison and he has gotten out of jail more plain than before, with an additional key, with an additional whiplash. On this wound many pour salt over and over again, that's why it will never close. On the other hand, curing it would mean deeply reflect on the sadness of humankind, a sorrow so deep.'

Tombstone

I come in and out of your body with such perfection of events, as if I were a molecule burning with feeling.

I love you.

But more than that I care about you, because you are something so real and pure, and especially something mortal, which moves me.

Which woman doesn't know her man is mortal? Which woman doesn't want to immortalise her love so that her lover will never die? Which woman doesn't challenge God and the laws of the earth to walk the green carpet of hope? Which woman has never loved the dead?

There are women who deny they have tombstones weighting on them.

Yet they keep opening secret tombs and burying themselves together with shadows from the past to pull out of it, with Egyptians, Assyrians and Babylonians, vases of art and gold.

The woman is so dear to the Lord for this arrogance and continuous charity. She who, with her delivery, wets the earth with blood as if she were an eternal martyr; she who is not afraid of fire; she who keeps harassing nature to find the medical herb which will keep her love and its perfect nudity alive.

The woman is a sphinx, she will never tell anyone she has vowed herself to silence, she will never tell anyone she has vowed herself to death.

Sink

I had an idea of scaring a neighbour of mine with an anonymous phone call. I had planned to tell her exactly the following: 'Blood from your sink.'

To be honest, I didn't understand the connection between blood, sink and toilet. Yet something had to be there nonetheless. I think this woman would moisten the dead with her saliva; maybe she would lick them, maybe she had beheaded a frog.

In fact the connection was actually there. As any other madness, the story of the sink too had its own logic.

This woman wanted to imitate me, just like the frog from the story who compared herself with the ox. Until she exploded miserably.

I could not confess the reason of the neighbour's death. Yet I am sure many guessed it.

Bed

I rest now, as always, from the long exertion of the day. Mediated and sudden exertion, exertion of muscles and of thought.

I am sitting on the edge of the bed thinking that today I will not make it.

But then your gaze arrives, before your voice, oh beautiful nude.

You sit next to me, unseen, and arm your wise hand with the old distaff. The bold rhyme, which is mine, stings itself in your presence.

You are a sublime emerald tip, but, after you, I forget and fall into the deep sleep of him who is close to you. And I ask myself how come this big flowery tripod, which is my bed, keeps changing its looks.

Yet he, my young groom, my adolescent, my pure, why doesn't he close my eyelids once and for all? Why doesn't he do like the god Eros who ran away from Psyche so as not to be seen?

He loves you, in my mind he sees your presence and he dreams of you, sees your womb and trembles, because it is a nursery of songs.

He sweats shame and love in deep incest. Meanwhile the sinister figure of the spy appears. The death goddess who takes the distaff in your stead and wraps it into black veils for forgetfulness.

You, blond fairy, have now finally had my groom, and it was him you wanted to marry, his fertile mind. Meanwhile you leave me and betray me once more. You will always betray me.

Books

I have abandoned books because they have been the greatest companions of my life; they were stronger than love, stronger than feeling, stronger even than children.

I have left my men for books because I had to become a great author and that was a categorical imperative. It's not that I was ambitious, I was simply someone with the vocation to write, who wanted to see in print the incorporeal fingers of books.

The fingers of books are very loving; the poets feel them, and are themselves loved by the books they create. No one knows if they will follow them; books are children who go their own way and marry other people.

Thus you become mother of a multitude of people from where a new genius will be born.

You hope in this, but you are also afraid you will have to compete with them.

Linen

Dear Federico, unlike all the troubles in the world, a bit hairless, a bit bald, a bit full of inner hair, a bit pensive, a bit dead, livened up by I don't know which wine. How much do you drink in a day?

This is slander I know, you never get drunk, but you would like to, like all the virtuous people who never sin and are inebriated by it.

Such misfortune has happened to you: that you are pure but are always mistaken for a fraudster.

Do you know, Federico, that the greatest fraudsters we've had were among saints and the greatest thinkers among naïve people? You could even commit a sin of just pure thought and no one will ever welcome you anymore, despite your baldness, your solitary cobra and the fact that you declare to be knowledgeable.

Culture is the best grain. Yet after having made pure little bundles out of it, you would rather be on the grass and softly knit your eyelashes in a childish state of abandonment to not feel like men, to not feel like women. Growing up is so hard, Federico.

I know you have already grown up in the past, I know you have gone beyond and then you have come back, because going further is not convenient to anyone anyway. Becoming a genius gives you a deep feeling of cold, it's like becoming a solitary cliff without even the flight of a bird, without even a rose garden of your own.

I was fine among the linen of the asylum, I will keep on saying it.

There wasn't any tragic sweat, rather, to tell you the truth; you would never sweat at all, you didn't go through this humiliating exertion. There wasn't even a seed of Venus around.

Venus was never born, has never had a beginning, yet she lives all the same. She is a ruin, a roaming voice, the sweetest reasonless hell.

You will never be able to find the beginning of Venus: she was born from the sea foam, and it's not easy to find her, because she trickles away, because she is transparent, because she is unstable.

Yet in the asylums, Federico, Venus was visible, Venus would show.

She would sit among us and she would tell us of old mythologies of the past; she used to say she had been abducted by a very fresh and seemingly benevolent mother. The elders of the Olympus would feel a lot of tenderness for her. Yet not Christianity, which had her labelled as a girl like any other, with few cards and many deceits. Christianity condemned this gentle girl imbued with motherly madness.

So that she ended up passing away between the hands of a friar or a jurist.

Maybe she died because she was too weak, or maybe too hasty.

Yet the mother with the heavy and flourishing hips still remains, the mother who is still looking for her, desperately looking for her.

Hands

I have spoken with my hands at length: on the keyboard, on the cheeks of babies, on the lover's body. Sometimes I embellish them with nail polish or with stratospheric rings so as to show that their tiredness is only a trick.

Hands are the soul of humankind. They are our personality. To educate a hand means to educate silence. There are creatures who have raised their hands to rejoice, others to defend themselves from violence. Someone has used their hands to bring justice, someone else to pray. Yet everyone has brought silence upon their hands.

I remember the hands of my father especially.

I have never seen any more beautiful than his, nor neater, nor more tapered. My father dedicated entire hours to his manicure. State employee and then bank director, he had to have very sensitive and private hands. With his hands my father would taste the money bills to feel the filigree.

He was the one to teach me to love paper, to value its worth and its predisposition to writing.

Every time my father would caress me I would fall in love with him.

Marilyn

The pretty and stimulating Marilyn Monroe, the myth of the picture house, was a decent and sensitive poet. Underneath the clichés about the diva only capable of showing her legs she hid a sensitive and deeply shaken soul.

For years she had been obsessed by the fear of ending up mad like her mother. I know well the secret games of certain women and certain doctors, I experimented them on my own skin. I wonder, however, which and how many psychological disasters poor Marilyn has fallen into.

Nevertheless I have formed an opinion about it. I am convinced that this splendid creature was simply mad with happiness, with love of life. Some people wanted to take her to pieces, certainly not because she had anything to do with the secret services, but because a pure soul is inconvenient. Men saved her from destruction. Because they were the only ones who guessed how she was joyfully child-like. So she became immortal. Marilyn's death was a death for love.

Milan

The fog creates Milan and Milan creates the fog. Between these fragments of darkness and these mirrors of light, always unmatchable, the spire rises.

When people from Milan go away from the Duomo, they carry the spire in their heart, and it hurts, it stings, and it devours them. It's their spirit of love.

You cannot not love Milan.

Milan is a bad mother, she runs after us with those old slippers of hers, with confetti in her eyes, with those bony hands, with those strange, huge, cobbled streets.

The refrain of an old song comes to mind: 'Via Filangieri is all made of stones, all night I've punched it and crunched all its bones.' And indeed Milan is all like that: punches and crunches. Via Filangieri, San Vittore, the prisons, the asylums, common abuses.[23]

Someone Flew Over the Cuckoo's Nest also comes to mind; the scene where the man who wanted to free all the mad people takes them out on a boat. It is exactly like that. Once the discharged patients would be put on a boat, pushed along the Naviglio. They were cripples, half-wits, disfigured people, unwanted, rejected by the citizens.

This cruelty has always happened, yet Milan has a heart which doesn't tolerate inhumanity for long, she is kind. Because Milan is a land on water, a big island of solidarity and tiredness, of goodwill and discouragement.

Milan's depression is caused by fog, which hisses, and turns into a sneeze, that fog which goes straight into the lungs and almost comforts them. A vast smoke, a vast London smoke.

---

[23] San Vittore is a prison in the city centre of Milan. Via Filangeri is the road in front of the prison [TN].

Milan is thirsty for this smoky gas, this poison which rises from promiscuous mouths, from wide open mouths hanging in mid-air, which want to breathe this unrepeatable fog. It is an illusion that it has been good air that has sustained us thus far.

Monologue

'There are vain people, lacking fear, who feel the wrist of the world, who look for joy inside the veins of the world, who come and go from the windows of dreams, dreams like mine.

People who parade their guts around at dawn, to show others their best reserve. It is maybe people who are wearing eternal boots.

Yet I, who do not have shoes, have climbed the mountain of her pleasure and I have known her. She had felt and seen much suffering and believed herself to be something which doesn't repeat itself. Instead, she was a passionate hydra, she was mount Sinai personified: looking at her I would see madness and a deserted crowd. I would see her inner wrinkles and her old age.

I have died at dawn, like a bee who sacrifices herself on a flower. Satisfied simply by glimpsing at her heart.

I have died empty, like a container from which everyone has drunk.

Sometimes I still knock at her door, but she, thinking me dead, doesn't even open. And doesn't notice that I, like a ghost, vibrate between her things. She blames everyone for moving her objects, but I am the one who still soils her house and plays pranks on her.

I asked God when I could have her in my arms again and he understood. Yet he also replied: "For now, because she has never been an angel, she too thinks you're just absent-minded."'

Death

You are not beautiful neither spiritual, yet tonight, coming back in my cab, I tried to speak to you and saw that after all you are an accessible creature. Yes, it's true, you don't listen to the soul, but you pay attention to the mind.

I haven't asked you why you are so scary, I've understood that you are as sweet as any other earthly creature. Surely you aren't an angel and neither a demon, you are something unusual.

People imagine you as a skeleton with two quite foul-mouthed jaws. But is it actually all true? Is it not possible that people represent tragic figures to fill their imagination?

Tell me if there is more tragedy in death or in life?

Yet after all I don't think you worry about these things; you are so cold, distracted. You sit next to the first stranger you happen to see, maybe just to get warm with their forgiveness. You want to be forgiven too, don't you, my friend? You want to be consoled for being so unhappy, lonely and self-sufficient, because no one calls you. The question is you don't like people's turmoil.

Now and then you rest and look at whoever shares their sleep with yours, whoever stays enchanted in front of you as if in front of a beautiful woman.

Ugly as you are, even you will make men fall in love with you.

Ugly as you are, even you will make poets sing.

Cigarette butts

I have gathered many in the asylum and I keep doing so – if there aren't any, I make up some new ones. The other day I called a cleaning company to brush them all away.

I never use the ashtray, because I am a very lazy person.

And I would like to tell those who bemoan widowhood that my husband, extremely tidy in life, has finally stopped pushing himself to be neat. I won't tell you what happened.

Navigli

Have you ever thought, Guido, of hiding in the night?

Imagine if you were to wear a crimson cape and pretend to be a thief and you tried to escape through these lousy courtyards along the Naviglio, where furniture of all sorts lays: discarded mattresses, old armchairs.

Once, Guido, the Naviglio was the location of craftsmen: they would stuff chairs and they would even sell poor kids. Everything was licit, everything was expected.

There isn't a thing on the Naviglio which hasn't had its crazy solution, its nightly flagrancy. Friars who would go there in secret to lust after young widows; girls kissing alongside the stream, cameras and old crinolines.

The great poets dying of anger and hard work, and these lagoon barges of a Venice that has nothing to do with old Meneghino and Cecca[24], who would go by in each other's arms, vain and vague puppets of this old Naviglio.

After all, Guido, I am slacking off, I am seen as a hopeless being; a surly poetess with her soul full of death.

It's hard, Guido, to live in two different sectors and always speak to the same person, which is me, which is you, my castellan, my secret lover.

You know that when one is close to the end, one doesn't confide love's secrets to death. Here's something that imbecile will never be able to know: how her victim has lived and how she has died – with the best audacity in the world, with the flag lifted on the pole of freedom.

And because death doesn't exist, it is only right that in order to deny her one starts to love.

---

[24] Meneghino and his wife Cecca are two traditional characters of the Italian *commedia dell'arte*, associated to the city of Milan [TN].

She doesn't know, the whiny, the shameless, the savage, that inside the mind there is a leaf so thin, a membrane so querulous it will always manage to defend itself from her turnaround.

It's the dialectics, Guido; never were philosophers more needed than nowadays, they never managed to teach us the triple deadly backflip of slyness.

Yet the most extraordinary slyness overlooking eternity is, nonetheless, always love. Even though you like to surround yourself of the splendour of your time, I believe in the reincarnated souls, in those who know a lot, not about history, but about the vast ashes of all the centuries. I do not dare to disappear before telling you what scares me: seeing centuries with all their lies forgotten.

Surely I will go back to being your pupil, or something that leans on your side like a main tree. Because you are the yard of my short, concise breath always approaching death.

Nocturne

Once, from Rome, you improvised a nocturne on the phone for me. I don't remember now, to be honest, whether it was night or dawn. Nocturnes are easy as life, they flow away lightly. They move the threads of desire, make them accustomed to the place, twirl them slowly around the stars.

Look. Between my hands I now hold a baby chrysalis, a firefly to whom I secretly dedicated your song, because I am too old to hear it. It's a fluorescent insect, a tiny being that slowly transcribes my verses, convinced I am the one who comes up with them. She still hasn't figured out I am a liar.

Yet she is a conscientious firefly, she carries out her job like a diligent fairy, and she makes you promises knowing she'll never keep them.

Your *sonata*, your *adagio*, your reflections on love were of great value.

You play from Rome with your head veiled in dark tears. You are just a boy and don't know that the poet is like a deep cliff, the greatest abyss you could have ever seen.

I know you are afraid to look at me, I know the abyss upsets you. I know the two multifaceted faces of love would like to die drowning in a deformed curiosity.

Don't worry though; I don't want to lower you into my abyss to lift myself up to the sky.

On the other hand it wouldn't be possible: there is an unshakable agent in the reign of madness, an insurmountable barrier. It would never allow us to come together in an endless spring.

Let us leave deceit on the table, then, let's leave it there, together with a pointless pencil which won't write anymore anyway.

Glasses

As a child I had some sort of hysteria, because my eyes at one point, after the trauma of failing a year at school, started to throw a tantrum. I almost became blind; I grasped things but I couldn't read and the pages terrified me.

My mother advised me to fall asleep on books to see if their content would reach the mind directly without having to go through the eyes.

And in fact, at night, sleeping on books, weirdly enough I would manage to read them. And I read so many of them that I became a school of desire.

Once I met a nosy doctor who wanted to understand where that blindness came from. He didn't see, and maybe neither did I, that Homer had transmigrated into my heart and that Gaspara Stampa[25], abandoned by Count Collatino, would cry for her sad love inside me.

I was like an empty shell, through which history's greatest poets would come and go. And I sang with such diversity of sound that I managed to parrot all the past geniuses.

What was left of me was a body thirsty for life and my great enigma was this: why on earth, despite being a great poetess, men liked me so damn much.

---

[25] Italian Renaissance poet [TN].

Objects

Objects pure at heart, which light the distances of the day; objects to which I have told about my best troubles and my celebrations. Objects rarefied by the thrill; objects that I barely manage to find again every day on my way, as if they were pointing me towards a path full of words and shadows.

After all we burden ourselves with objects as if we were a mule; they become symbols of our failed destiny, they are charlatans trying to sell us a bled-dry folly of time.

Every object is a clock, an hourglass on which time has passed.

Everyone asks me of how many objects my house is made up, and of how many hours, of how many silences. Yet no one has ever realised that objects have a precariousness of their own, that they cannot die and that they will always be stereotyped and fake like our life.

Give me, oh soul, a painless birth, something which won't make me die. And repeat after me that litanies are equally distant from the feeling of an anguishing demolition.

Why does virtue sound like the composition of objects? And wouldn't it be stupid to give Guido anything that doesn't actually suit him, something which is damning both for him and for me? A scarlet bone; a skeleton of a baby that no one has ever seen; a harsh and noxious birth that belongs to the same object, which is nothing other than the longing of desire.

And here is the last muscle of our effort falling to the ground, gathering scattered, extinguished objects, objects which tell badly lived poems and which have the sense of endurance.

Shadow

Dialogue between a man and a woman.

A garden. A woman and a man meet. She looks at him ecstatically.

'Aren't you perhaps the prince of a new Eden?'

'I am just a heap of ground with some sweet spikes of memory.'

'If I am not mistaken you have a triangular face like the one of him who hasn't found an inner balance.'

The man looks at her: 'You are using a word that doesn't belong to me. A word that never belongs to two people when they are hopelessly alone in a desert.'

'Which is your desert?'

'I could tell you it's loneliness, but it's not true. The fact itself that I am a ball of thoughts and nerves and that I do not accept life makes me think myself a defector. I miss the law. Something dark, worn out, obscene. A sudden certainty, like that of a shot in the head.'

'Are there wire fences here?'

The man smiles: 'In this desert that is partly mine and partly yours I am looking for something. I am looking for a shadow. Mine.'

The woman: 'My shadow is so faithful to me! Even more, I'll tell you, they have taught me to call her angel. A long guardian angel with endless wings. Why did you say we are in the sands of Eden?'

'Because heaven is fluid, but what distinguishes heaven from earth is precisely the lack of shadows.'

'Has your shadow maybe fallen off on the ground?'

'Yes, but it didn't make a noise. And this created loneliness in me.

There are people complaining, people losing frills and desires, people losing their own door, their own entrance, their own house.

Yet I, as I have told you, have lost the time of the shadow.

I'll tell you I had built it only with my memory and I had demanded she'd never lose sight of me, that she'd be good as my disposition and, above all, that she wouldn't be some form of groundless stupidity.

Yet she betrayed me and all my keen goodness went lost.

Now, it's my soul that is evil and I am the eternal Abel looking for his King.

I do not know the Bible and neither do I know the beginning of art, but I know that a person's shadow is the model of his imagination and this soul now rebels against me and it's the darkest witness I have ever seen; the most unstable, the most extensive.

A useless steamer which knows thousands alleyways and goes so far from my darkness.

If you knew, woman, that darkness is not shadow and that you too, with your straight blond hair, could be darkness, an ill-concealed punishment.'

'You want to kill me? Then why don't you?'

'I am telling you I have no dimension, no events, no hope and you are laughing of my eyes.

You find me exuberant, maybe divine, and while I tell you of my shadows you smile.

No one has ever told me what a woman is and, after all, you could be any cat or a lifeless butterfly.

But I don't want to touch you, because to me the Shadow matters more than you.

That Shadow I have lost in a leaf of wind.'

Clock

Time is life's greatest grace, yet to stay long in a hospital you need firstly to lose the cognition of it. Doctors are in the habit of asking the patient: 'What day is it today?', 'How old are you?', and whether you know that the interval between when you get one pension allowance and the next is of two months.

For regular people, instead, time is a wonderful invention; Cronos lived in it excellently. All the alarm bells have declared to people that it was a certain time; even Dracula would rely on clocks.

Immanuel Kant served for years the shopkeepers of his neighbourhood: whenever they saw him come out they'd regulate their clocks.

My father too had a personal regulator. To set his clock he would put his ear near its face as if to hear the pulses of a heart. And we all were surprised by those tolls echoing through the big walls, carrying a sense of forgiveness and adoration towards the mystery of life.

Those beautiful verses by Quasimodo come to mind, where he's praying death not to ever touch the alarm in the kitchen, where his mother lives.

That white polish which has varnished our lives for years, which has established our timetables, which has sent us to sleep, which has woken us up and which has even told us it was time for poetry.

Everything moved almost unbeknownst to us, on the great landscape of the clock.

I, however, prefer the hourglass with that sand running swiftly from one little vial to the other. Between those grains our childish eyes would bloom like big anemones when the hourglass would be put at the centre of an ample table, as if it were one of the seven wonders. And we kids would pray dastardly or naively that the passage of time would be slow, ever slower, because the sand had some golden reflections.

And life flows just the same, like sand, with many specks of gold inside.

Yet it's the meridian the most beautiful clock I have ever seen, because you don't need any gear to ask the sun when it's time for life and when it's time for death. I use the word death to mean rest as well. It is then that it gets quiet.

I don't usually ask God for forgiveness, I know I get up unconsciously, live unconsciously and write unconsciously. I have lost count of the days. But I feel so loaded up with years, I feel so old and unhappy now that I don't understand why my secret clock sometimes tells me it's time to love.

Pages

As a child I had a big collection of books. I have read so many I would turn to ashes on them. I would devour them, suffer them, but I loved them so much that to a man I would have definitely preferred a book.

I have bought them, catalogued them, showcased them, held them in my heart. I would close my eyes dreaming of culture.

Still today, when I fall asleep is because I have found a good book. And when the book is not there my night is anguished.

Nonetheless I have learnt a trick now: sometimes I buy an unread book and I put it under the pillow, thinking I will read it at night. My craving for reading makes it penetrate me, like your body, Ernesto. I become a man who loves a woman, the book. The book is a great fairy. I cannot love you, Ernesto, because I sleep on books, which don't have blood. If I were to put my ear to your heart instead, I would hear the pulse of life and it would bring me far away. However, I love the pages you have yet to write to me and I wish you would write them for me.

You will never be a poet, Ernesto, until you'll send love letters to the great lover of books.

Bench

Benches don't absorb anyone's sweat; you should never go on them to die.

Yet my latest lover died there, neglected by everyone. The hate of mankind poured out upon him. My lover died alone.

People are a horrid mixture of unhealthy appetites and torn egotism – what Spagnoletti[26] used to call the consideration of the private.

The charity reserved to Titan wasn't only for him, because in him and in his poverty resided the divine hand. No one ever understood this. Kissing a poor means kissing God, father David used to say that too.

Yet God is present in the rich as well, wealth is a divine gift too. Then why do men swear at each other?

The bench is a piece of wood, and the eternal Pinocchio sleeping on it could unexpectedly turn into one too. Pinocchio will never have flesh, nor a devil inside because he doesn't have a house, so he will never be considered a citizen. Yet no one considers that the true house of humankind is the world.

---

[26] Giacinto Spagnoletti, Italian literary critic, poet and writer of the 20th century [TN].

Bread

Bread has always inspired me. Its legend began in the post-war period, when people were struggling to get a hold of white bread.

Now some people throw it away as if it was rubbish. Yet it was the symbol of knowledge and of the hearth. The communion was made of bread dipped in wine – according to Jewish principles it meant 'collective dining', or circle of disciples. The traveller who was supposed to bring The Good News to everyone, from house to house, would eat bread too.

There is also the bread of culture. Many are hungry for culture and many don't have bread. The great, especially the great editors, take care of feeding these bellies. I have often investigated how the vague feeling of sadness comes to be: maybe, almost certainly, it's a consequence of the fact that people are hungry for culture and thirsty for knowledge.

I remember nunneries where bread was disciplined, asylums where bread was banned and I remember my mother who every morning would put a freshly-made loaf of bread in my rucksack, and that was supposed to last all day.

Bread dipped in oil, eaten slowly to make it last longer, bread crumbled on the sheets in moments of great tension. The bread of lovers and the wonderful bread of forgiveness: the intimate look in the daily bread.

Mussolini used to say: 'Love the bread, joy of the hearth.' And that is how he, like an authoritarian visitor, came and went from our mouths as a source of inspiration.

Word

Laura, you meet foul words; words without future and without a moral joy, words which have known the dirt of revenge and which have raised with forward-looking hands against the walls of dreams.

The asylum is the only kind of social life I have ever known, where many scattered melodies would sing together their innate generosity.

Generous were the souls bulging with pain, with their belly full of the juices of melodies. Generous were those who would carry useless burdens up and down the hills of their greatness and would scatter them like chaff in the wind. Generous were their tired inebriation and those colourless hands carrying heavy bricks full of happy childhood.

Generous were those souls warmed with wind, oh yes, generous like pure honey.

And I have unkindly left that oasis of peace where everything was good and purified by the cold of a burning heart.

Those elders there were made of fear alone. I remember that in any day you could lift the layer of their eternal friendship to find a corpse inside, and remove the colour of their extreme face without them showing not even a hint of death or fear.

I remember every day a wound would be healed and that every day corresponded perfectly to the next, that each border was filthy with truth.

I have tasted the happiness of life and the layer of sadness that breathed death in. Yet those elders and those young suitors on the floor – because their spasms were atrocious – would give hints of luxury to the demons, to the reprobates who enjoyed the acerbity of those faces visited by madness.

Madness is therefore an eternal visit, it never sleeps, it pulses of a becoming without beginning. You can look for the origin of the world, yet not for the origin of madness, which is without beginning, which breaks the borders of desire and which rips off the leaves of others.

The white hair of the asylums' windows was the finger of God pointing at the faith in the invisible redemption of humankind.

I call horrible the sign above me that speaks me of inhumane pain. I call cold the papers touching my thoughts and restraining them inside the conceited halo of disgrace.

I curse that radiant blushing of shame that covered me years back at the Vergani[27], where I got dressed in cold rags to satisfy the greed of the man living to the side of my window and that of his woman, powerful only with sin and with ignoble exploitation.

I curse the world that welcomes those unbearable sins. They are worms with sophisticated faces, wetting the virginal womb with sperm.

When the doors of the prison opened I got thrown in the only real asylum: life.

---

[27] Psychiatric hospital in Taranto [TN].

Delivery

My father had severely forbidden me to read medicine textbooks and those which blatantly showed scenes of deliveries.

Because at the time I was following a History course, I knew the Parti[28] were an ancient population that had fought against the Romans; peculiar people, no more than that.

I have then learnt at my expenses, paying for the ignorance of my youth, that puns help us a lot to overcome misunderstandings.

So, having realised that doctors don't know much, I have tried too to fight my war. Yet my battle was not for the conquest of a land, rather for the conquest of a son.

It's the same terrible battle I am fighting now to have you, Ernesto.

---

[28] Also the Italian word for delivery [TN].

Pastina[29]

I love Maria Corti[30] a lot, despite her robe and the academic touch.

I remember Maria when she was young, newly graduated, and like a freezing sparrow chick she would stay at Mrs Mustorgi's, in a small boarding house with a large sofa. She had such a tormented and thoughtful face that I liked her right away.

She was certainly my first teacher; it was she who brought Manganelli to me so that he would educate me. Looking at the two of us Maria would shake her head, saying we were crazy.

She was already so wise then that Manganelli and I entrusted her with our destiny and our life.

Maybe Maria Corti could not be a mother, yet she was mother of many disciples, often very generous, sometimes too strict.

Still now, when a strong feeling of love for her comes over me, I call her at eight o'clock at night. And she shouts at me: 'I have told you a thousand times I am eating my *pastina* at this time of night.'

---

[29] Small sized pasta [TN].

[30] Italian philologist, literary critic, and novelist of the 20th century [TN].

Piper

This book, Chicca, seems endless. My great far away lover – I am talking of Guido – kidnaps children, I don't know how, like the Piper.

His is an atrocious revenge, because he manages to take away the child in me. And the child desperately runs after him.

I was telling an old lover of mine that the life of the elders is a continuous evolution and that, when they can't take it anymore, they go to the children to learn how to grow up. Because we forget that at any time of day a strange Piper could summon us. And we always hope it isn't death.

Easy Poem

A guy used to say life is like a fallen woman
Who grabs hold of young damsels
With her deceitful falsity.

A guy who had vowed himself to horrid greatness
Used to say life is like a vineyard
And you need to cultivate it well
With hands full of harmony.

Maybe he was finally speaking the truth
Yet he did not say life is fast
More than a hare inside a forest.

Poet

I believe in the nourishment of the world; oh you who is a hedge, and tells me of the eternal centuries.

I believe in your painless mouth, in your teeth white as coral, in your boyish hand. In your prosperous breast, despite your being a man, and in your cruel eyes scrutinising me.

You have destroyed me in a second, so young and beautiful, and you've told me to go and hide because I had been repeating myself for too long.

Yet you, with your utter newness, remind me of a badly lived, dull, almost alcoholic childhood.

A blunt childhood where they would always speak of war victims, heroes, victories, fascist cries, abstinence, enrolments and houses collapsing. They have bombarded my soul, slowly slowly they have broken my stones, which were my old kneeling-stools, the stones where I would go looking for the bread tree.

This is what love is: something that doesn't see your swelling, something that doesn't see you've already become a mummy.

And thus the old discipline calls you. You want to be like that Berenice who has the eyes wide as the world, and who is substantially horrendous.

You show me legendary buttocks and a flourishing chest against which, I don't know why, I would point Hitler's weapons to make a hero out of you.

Yet you insist on being a poet and that's a different thing then. This stubbornness of not having enemies, of not looking for them.

I encourage you, my son, to abandon poetry, because you could cry.

Could you ever love me? Me, who is looking at you, who is the poetry, and who, as you can see, is old, toothless and tired and maybe an alcoholic. Yet you summon me, want to speak to me, want to know from me what an elegiac couplet is. I know elegies, not couplets, and I reject you, because I, poetry, do not want to inhabit you. Otherwise I would whip you to death, otherwise I would show you my breathlessness and the great, colossal murders I have committed for someone else.

Do you want to imitate me? Do you want to smear yourself like me and still keep a beautiful body like in *The Portrait of Dorian Grey*? Beware, the danger is that in the long term the writer becomes as much of a criminal as the demon who keeps him with him; something as swift as a glance.

You are an honest man so don't look at me; there are things I am hiding from you and great inhospitable pleasures. She could love you, the calumny impersonated. She could devour your bones, make you cry, take your favourite weapon from you.

Don't look at me, you don't know what I'm hiding from you, and more than anything don't look back. You could find that behind your back there are words and wordless borders and especially the damning proof that she's a thief like me, that she will beat your buttocks up, strip them for the infamous monthly puncture which will make you drunken with nothingness.

You appear to me in the night and you are scalped, raptured for the eternity by the conquest of a noble Indian. Abandon the house of the Usher, walk away through rundown streets. They will surely be less wicked than this house which has no memory anymore.

Door

About Raboni[31] I will only say a few words. That one day, I don't know why, I ran to his house at exactly midday and I rang the doorbell. I needed to see him, to speak to him about poetry. However he told me: 'Please, I eat at this time of day.' Since that day I have never knocked at his door again.

---

[31] Giovanni Raboni, Italian poet of the 20th century [TN].

Priest

'If I put a woman against the sky she walks free as a girl. Now that I am far away I understand that to her, so tiny and lost, I must have looked like a Cerberus in the flesh. The man who wanted to scare her childhood.

'I've coloured myself in cold. And I keep living in allotments of faith, where healthy herbs for gastritis grow, herbs for some sorts of long-life elixir.

'Yet my faith is not scorching as it once was. My faith has now died.

'A dawn like anyone else's has come for me; I have "redeemed", shall we say, myself. I have healed from her love, I have reabsorbed myself into myself.

'Yet when I loved her I was like an overflowing season, I had become the Red Sea.

'I have given her my silt and she has given me flowers of a song in return.

'I know, I couldn't write with her next to me. She was poisoning my soul, she was like a herb exploding in my blood, she was the warmest venom I had ever drunk, she was made of earth and fire.

'I, who had always feared faith, was reduced to madness because of her.

'Alas, after her I have never had faith again.'

Cobwebs

Cobwebs have been adorning my walls for years: they are a haze of light, a haze of dust. They don't sadden me, but I don't understand them.

I don't understand why the dust from the furniture went to settle itself so high up, so much so that I refuse to look at it; others see it because they pay attention, used as they are to coherent cleanliness, to vases of myrrh on the tables.

Instead, what worries me is that I can't catch sight of the spiders.

Once they used to say that these tiny little animals brought luck. Yet now there aren't any more spiders, of parasites instead there's plenty.

The spider brings cheerfulness; he's a seer, a poor. And especially a great catcher: almost every time the fly lets herself be seduced and eaten, as I have done with the many lovers of my past.

Palace

I have gotten used to sweeping the house like a Cinderella waiting for a fairy to knock at the door and show me the way to the castle.

I use to live once in a palace full of spells, on a peak of the moon, a great palace with an evil fairy inside.

Who knows if the witch was actually my mother or the madwoman next door. Who knows if it was I who would turn into a servant or into a princess. This doubling, this being able to be both the slave and the mistress, doesn't maybe mean that you can serve both the devil and the grace?

Why do I live in this hovel now? Because I want to stay a Cinderella. Why do I look inhospitable and unkempt? Because I am waiting for your kiss.

Some unbalances become candour when a prince walks by distractedly and sees, beyond the mended rags of the patched mind, something warm and extreme.

Try to undress me, love, try to undress me.

Bra

Bras are a natural womanly lowness, which highlight the graces of the apocalypse. Their role, be they balconette ones or cup ones, is to lift what vulgarly falls.

The bra is playful and coquettishly and hints at the unfolding of everything. Its laces are improper; they are there to unleash hell.

Manganelli's hellish women, his lamb-shaped women have their origin in the bra. They show a natural pallor, a lack of consideration, a weakness devoid of any hostility. Yet, in fact, whoever unleashes a bra dies.

I keep money in my bra because I have the bad habit of making my lovers, who are my editors, pay me: each book, therefore, has costed me a bra.

A Rage of Love[32], on the other hand, has costed me getting sectioned into the asylum where, unfortunately, they took even my panties from me.

---

[32] 1989 work by Merini, *Delirio Amoroso*, translated in English by Pasquale Verdicchio (Guernica, 1996) [TN].

Wrinkles

Let me touch your pretty face and let me read childhood on it.

There are some marks, some traces of tears, some streams of wrinkles. I would like to ask you how many times you've cried or how many times you've smiled. I am convinced that since you were a kid your skin has been tensing in the spasm of duty towards life.

Do you believe, Guido, that a little boy has the duty to cry and die in his little games? Do you believe, Guido, that every child should forcedly raise to the height of the table and thus find out that to rest their chin on it they have to let out the first wrinkle?

They don't realise, absorbed as they are in the anxiety of catching the secret of our face, that by growing up they'll start to wear, gradually, the mask of silence. They don't know, Guido, that they're horribly throwing up their soul and losing it day by day. Until they'll become like us: an apparently cheerful mask, often very fake.

Isn't it true that when you come home in the evening, and I come home, we rip off from our face this miraculous skin and we tiredly hang it to a wall?

Isn't it true, Guido, that when we collapse at night on the edge of the bed we take each other's heads in our hands and we say: 'Neurosis is just a divine suspect'?

And what if it was a certainty? What if these wrinkles weren't our past but only the identikit of a mad future that has already declared us dead?

The person behind these thin walls that sometimes are our hands, the person threading on the silent grass of their own sins, knows the world unknowingly and endlessly repeats within himself the monosyllables of his childhood to reduce the wrinkles, to adequately define a face they do not like, a face which is only appearance of matter or dragon mask. The poetry missed during the day, something that will never happen.

Because, after all, neither me nor you, nor the silent imbecile who brushes against us on the street, nor the man in chains, nor the pretty girl appearing in the sun can count on one's own mask. And even if we had a smooth and perfect face we would want to draw these wrinkles with prowess, because they attest our power and the few things we have experienced in life.

Many people, many malevolent insects have walked over our wrinkles, yet when we'll be old we'll become like rosy and scented children absolutely devoid of signs. Unfortunately only God knows why the soul doesn't know anguish.

Shoes

My worn, dirty, shabby shoes.

The Red Shoes, here's a film I have seen over and over for years. My red shoes have been my poetry. I have danced for a long time, up until exhaustion, on that same string.

My ugly shoes, my holed shoes.

If I enter a shop they immediately look at my shoes. I understand and declare that I am indeed able to pay. To which they smile and bring out the goods. Behind the counters of the shops there are respectable people, focused ladies.

But I am a child, I get in and say: 'I want that and nothing else.' That 'I want' scares them; they're afraid I'll rob them. This reminds me of that joke about that guy that went to the bank with an assault rifle. The cashier asked him: 'Cash in?' And he replied: 'No, cash out!'.

The opposite happens to me. Only once a shop clerk gave me a nice dress and a new hat for free. Yet then she specified: 'They're not for you, but for the great memory of Paolo Volponi[33].'

---

[33] Italian writer of the 20th century [TN].

School

Chicca, I write to you once more, my love, you who is injectable like a fresh syringe.

Thus, tree of my nuts, I see you singing beyond the hedge of my memories which are looking for you.

I have opened a school for women only, where in the warmest hours Sappho dances, in the time I fall back in love with him.

And then I tell you of my desires and my temptations, and of how I am simply afraid.

Oh dear, I don't know why I associate your image to his. You're both young, you'd be good together, while I, old as I am, am remorseful of your feelings.

Alas, such a long road to walk for the pause of a single face.

You too angel, defeated every night, rest in me, my secret lover.

Woods

Back in the day I was really moved by *The Yearling*. I was moved by that child who wanted to protect the abandoned fawn. It's hard to raise a deer, it's hard to take him away from the beauty of the woods, hard to separate him from fear.

When a man loves he shakes like a fawn, and whoever picks him up, in a gesture of love, doesn't realise this pup could die. Yet women's hands have healing virtues; they know the woods are not everything there is, that fear is not everything there is.

Dante too finds himself in a dark wood where everything is scary and noisy and there's no light to be seen.

And thus once, a long time ago, I met a young lover. He moved me; I thought I could have kidnapped him, I could have taken him away from that big deception that is his solitude.

Quasimodo says: 'Everyone stands alone on the heart of the earth', and it is well true. In the face of death there will be no father or mother, nor in the face of happiness, nor in the face of love.

We find ourselves to be needing to make a decision on our own, when we're still pups. Because sixty year old pups do exist.

What the child in the book wondered is whether it would be right to take the fawn away from his fear, from his great woods. But then he decided and made the mistake, broke the maternal rule.

Yet when I fell in love with you and found you so young I didn't ask others for advice. I came to your grave, mother, and I asked you in tears: 'Mum, will you let me bring this puppy home?'

Cigarettes

I smoke a lot. Once I used to smoke way less, I would lit a cigarette and pass it to my husband, who died smoked out. Meanwhile I had a lot of things to take care of: cleaning, ironing curtains, looking after the kids.

A book which I have always found a good read is *Doll House* by Ibsen: I was a bit like Nora too, only, with time, my husband had started to consider both me and my children as dolls to exhibit. Until one day the chain of grace broke.

Nora did not want a father, but a husband, and she left slamming the door. The kids got a bit frightened, but understood right away and immediately took their lives in their own hands – they were conscientious and flew far away.

To whomever asks me why I ended up in an asylum I can now give my answer: I had met a man who had understood my need to live.

Sleep

Rarely now I manage to sleep and rarely I can find the calm. But when I sleep I dream and dreams are the sweetest melody of the universe.

During sleep we reinvigorate ourselves and when we are able to dream then we reach absolute perfection. Even during nightmares we are finally in peace, even though we drag our own enigmas. There are enigmas in life that are given back to us in dreams, that are arranged as clean clothes in the sun.

I have stayed a child because I have had the ability to dream and to see like in a mirror that I have had and almost perfect existence. As far as dreams are concerned, that is, not as far as agony is.

I don't pray anymore, yet God has left me dreams and in dreams, thank God, I don't see any lovers nor editors anymore, nor even myself. I only see the pleasure of the image, and nothing can ever hurt me again. Images run fast on a secret video, as if they were operated by a crank handle of the brothers Lumière. A cinema of my own. I only wake up when I realise that what is operating that handle is the hand of Pier Paolo Pasolini[34].

---

[34] Italian film director, poet, writer, and intellectual [TN].

Mirror

I have been looking at myself in the mirror for years. It's a fragile mirror, manifold, interchangeable; a mirror which doesn't live in any place and any time, which isn't a synonym either of time or of place: it's the multiple mirror of my conscience and maybe of yours too.

The mocking sneer is the same as any theatre mask. Sometimes it opens into wide meadows, sometimes it speaks to me of graves.

All the women of this life and yourself, who are next to me, now have looked into my mirror.

It's not the mirror of fear, it's not the mirror of hunger. It is neither the mirror which darkens the most subconscious desires. Yet you blond girl, who have two perfectible hands, uncertain breasts and maybe perceptive legs, you know well that mirrors live in our words.

Many years ago I tried the pleasure of the first discovery: I was a young vagabond with a little bit of human dust who would gather great loves from the street.

And the mirror was beheaded.

It was unthinkable that next to that lean girl a tall simulacrum would rise and that the mirror would start to sing again. Yet I'll tell you that with the passing of the years I too made a pact with the devil and of that meagre haughty beauty nothing remained, truly nothing.

The devil, my girl, girl of jade constraints, only the devil could take possession of that great silver soul.

With time the mirror, because of the smell, of the disagreements, of the violent fights, started to distort. It became a limestone which resembled a wall without an opening, without an arch, even without the chance of a window or some appearance of void from which to jump.

So it became the mirror of health, a miserable health within which I measured my defeat. I finally felt in peace – now I could brush my hair without abandonment, no more trying to like myself, I could come up and down the stairs and by the cold banisters no more thinking that in my house there was this marble presence which kept giving out reflections.

When I was a child they used to say that the mirror is a symptom of evil and that you shouldn't fix yourself up and make yourself pretty in front of it, because beauty is a deadly trap.

The mirror is an absolute pyramid. I fear it as if it were a man capable of being enough for me, giving me a hunchback, making me uglier than I am. Because, believe me, no real beauty has ever been reflected in a mirror.

Now I ask you, beautiful girl, what link there is between the genius, the word and the mirror, and whether it would not be worth it to shatter it once and for all. Because whatever they say, the soul has its silver reflections too.

Sometimes I have seen in the mirror a stare that did not recognise me: the soul of the killer. I would have wanted to kill him for the sake of my love, in order to lust after the man whom I now love and who does not look at himself in the same memories as mine.

How he is I'll tell you right away: a paradise, a superb paradise of inadequate delight; a white nature in which the crystal of fear gets lost. Something that you, girl in love who lives like a rising stream, cannot understand. This is why I will never explain to you what music is.

If you want you can live in the same mirror as me and look at yourself together with me. Then you'll see that despite the passing of time I have remained a witch, a witch that is handing you the poison of my poetry, a witch who is wishing you would die. So that you, now living in my mirror, would never find an answer to my old age.

After all, this is the wish of someone who loves and is about to dissolve into nothing.

Statue

I often tell you, Emanuela, about my torments. At least you take them as such, and so do I. Yet maybe they're just passages of a life young and old that goes here and there, like a snake.

We live, -ish, a bit like rich people a bit like poor, a bit like big shots.

Now and then I even tell you of my loves. You listen carefully, deeply moved. Also because you don't understand their meaning. Though honestly neither do I.

And so I want to tell you something.

Many years ago I was about to buy a big statue an admirer of mine had offered me. It was a votive statue, it portrayed an half-naked woman flying towards the sky. I had called it Life.

It was the name of a woman I had seen butchered in a hospital in Taranto. Her last prayer had been: 'If you go to Milan, free me from this prison.'

In Milan I have found many other Lives who have grabbed on to my shreds of flesh and I haven't been able to save myself ever since.

Yet, Emanuela, I save myself with you. And with the memory that Michele Pierri and I once co-authored a book called *De Consolatione* [35].

Only one thing can heal life: life itself.

---

[35] Latin for 'On Consolation' [TN].

Roads

Roads are easily faced because they offer us paths that lead everywhere. Yet we also know that, however far they can guide us, they will always bring us back to the starting point. We walk away from home, from destiny, from our lover to go back to basic, return to the simplicity of our beginning, whether it be good or bad.

Now they are asking me to travel. Yet I don't even count the roads treaded anymore; they are recurrent roads, already suffered, already seen, already explored.

Once, with the help of my imagination, in front of the Sforza Castle I relived the whole magnificence of the Sforza. It was one of those raptures Raboni speaks of, one of those past lives, one of those happy reincarnations everyone has inside of themselves. I saw Alighieri face to face, and many others.

Years back I found out, for instance, that I had the same rhythm and the same way of speaking as Gaspara Stampa, the one who pined after her rueful love for Collatino da Collato. The great lovers who have crossed centuries have walked more roads anyone can imagine.

A sacred ECT saved me from the big artifice and then the great adventure with Joan of Arc started for me, so much so that I had to go into therapy. You'll find it odd, but at the time I had some terrible burns on my back that made me cry.

Doctor G. understood me and made me recount under hypnosis in the therapy session how Saint Joan had died. When I woke up I was surprised to see Milan. In any case, I still wear riding boots and put up a fight with anyone.

Rug

At this point I shiver at the thought of my health. Yet I don't understand, dear Ernesto, what this wave of happiness is that is pervading me without much doubt and pain. Is it you? Or is it a psalter of a nunnery I have never forgotten?

You tell me you're writing and that you'll become a great poet one day. So I cover my ears and say: 'Damn it, don't talk to me about poetry anymore.'

Why? Because I want to spare you my mirror, my combustions, and I want your eyes to sparkle only with silence.

To all poets I, like a model mother, recommend not to write, not to burn their lips in unworthy kisses, not to pick up the pen with that horrible tremor that pervaded me on the first day of school, not to change mothers, not to pretend to be old on the desks of the youth, not to quiver with expectations, not to go to exams with shredded and twisted shoes.

To all young people I recommend: open your books religiously, do not look at them superficially, because in them is contained the courage of our fathers. And close them with dignity when you have to take care of something else.

Still, more than anything else, love the poets. They have wandered the earth for you for many years, not to build tombs on it, or simulacra, but altars.

Think that you can walk on us as if on large rugs and fly past this sad everyday reality.

Taxi

There is a touch of divine in your eyes, Ernesto, a touch of juvenile merriment.

Maybe young people have finally found peace, that peace that makes them smile, that peace that makes them be good to the elders.

On this subject I am reminded of my love for Salvatore Quasimodo; those three delicate and sad years during which I never asked the master anything, other than to touch him.

Don't ask me whether I truly loved Quasimodo; you cannot love a poet, you can only sweat over him and cover him with the mantle of your youth so that he won't get cold, so that he won't be touched by evil.

My love for the Poet was a sort of reverential reserve, it was a yearning wait in the hope that he would read his last verses to me. It was going around ecstatically as if I had seen a saint or I had touched a big amulet.

To whomever rebukes me for taking a taxi, despite the cold and my old age, I remind the numberless taxis me and Quasimodo would hop on together.

He could not drive, even though he wished to be and appear like a great prophet. It was understandable after all. His house in Garibaldi Avenue was wonderful, one of the few still standing after the torment of the war.

A great and fiery poet, a great and passionate lover. Yet more than anything his smart and subtle irony comes to mind – his bitter smile of a person who can penetrate things and the mysteries of life.

I remember everything about him, even the smell of his shirt when, on an August night, I said goodbye to him.

He shouted that I was a wretch, that away from him I would have found myself face to face with misfortune.

It was true.

No ECT ever managed to destroy the memory of him. And those are miracles only poets can do.

Actress

Why do you, woman, stand on the most gossipy stage? Why do you learn, suffer, mimic and transform your joy into tears? Why do you throw yourself on the floor like someone possessed and rip your skin off and renounce your hymen of joy forever?

On the stage you let yourself be deflowered by everyone, you spread your legs as if endless trains were to depart from you, you are nothing more than a commercial station and a man without measure.

Because you, fresh and blessed theatre woman, manage to be many women in one, a single petal of words. Your tongue frets as if you had a short incinerator burning vividly at your feet. And you dance, you dance on the words like a tensed tail, and strangely the words come back to you and you flush them on the floor where they become alive and turn into fiery arms that hug your torments.

You are beautiful and obtuse like all angels, and like all angels you devour space.

Think of when Mary's angel appeared: an immense sheet of paper, a happy papyrus and Mary became a poet thanks to a wretched and grandiose gaze of love.

Yet you make theatre, you oil your skin, your soul becomes virtue and the axes flow down your feet as long tides.

And lo and behold we suddenly sense that the angel is there. From behind the curtain he wants to hint at the scene of suggestion.

And lo and behold he lays unsolved like a dead man, not having witnessed the mystery of scenic art. He, the paradise lost.

Yet you visibly look for the man with the flower in his mouth so as to hide from the public the fact that grace is not casual, that it is not just any refrain. The flower, yes. You are wearing the ring at your finger together with the atrocious doubt of not being pretty enough to interpret the angel wandering in space like a blind man eager to possess you. Certainly angels have as many eyes as peacocks do and use women to engrave poisonous verses in front of a fleeting curtain, a curtain which escapes our hands as the vigour of the verse does.

I know you are there. Be careful not to fall from your season, not to poison yourself beyond success, not to say for instance that a woman could simply be an umbrella or something that, having been successful on Earth, forgets its past.

The standing ovation in the theatre is something sublime, but so is failure.

If you sing and murmur like water, be sure many men and women will move with you in the space and in your depths.

Yet because you make theatre, try to fall rightly every night and to die coherently, since in spite of all the disasters, of all the deaths and all the torments people still want logic. And naturally logic is not in the space, nor even in the heart, yet maybe it is found in the precepts of music.

Learn, then, to choose your sheets and the many scores of your future. You can pull them out like heroes' swords and be sure you'll meet many ready to pick them up.

Web

Everyone thinks I am a great lover and in fact I am.

Yet every time I lay my hand on my plot someone undoes my web, as if I were a Penelope. Is there any logic in love anyway? Is there any logic in poetry? The only thing I know is that poetry needs to be seized in the moment, like thoughts, like images, before they get cold and become a stale dish.

Like so, a kiss delayed is like a sent back letter.

Telephone

On the phone I have created many books and many stories. With the phone I have gotten my whole life wrong, but I've also corrected it. The telephone gave life to my ghosts.

I have met and loved many men on the telephone. The phone is love made with moderation, a secret caress, a wish to hide one's own outpour of history. Through the phone I've deceived Ernesto too, because my voice can be young, and sometimes feebly bitter. On the phone I have enchanted and I've become disenchanted.

Yet why this secret shot to the heart? Why do you tremble, have a fever, feel sick? Because the phone doesn't answer you. He's gone away with another woman, away from your magic rituals, away from you, and forever it seems.

Then the phone rings and he reappears, though not to come back to you, only to call you once, twice, endless times.

TV

I would like to sit quietly in front of the TV and watch a film, but one of the old ones, like *Mrs. Miniver*, *The Song of Bernadette*, *Terminal Station*.

Terminal Station, indeed; it happened to me too to remain dazed, staring at someone who did not want to leave because I did not want to stay.

Dazed for hours, without being able to make a decision. Like so, no longer young, but rather quite old, Michele and I looked at each other enraptured.

A human and psychological drama without solution until, to fix things, just like in the film, a kid appeared and suddenly called me grandma and made me realise it was time to stop loving.

The poor Bernadette comes back to my mind too, she who, accused of dragging her leg around the convent, burst into tears. She couldn't keep the pace with the other novices. Thus, overcome by tiredness, she lifted her dress and showed them her sick legs. She hadn't said anything for many years because – one way or another – she could still stand.

The other day, while I was squawking through the streets of the Naviglio, a neighbour of mine told me: 'You can walk, you're luckier than me.'

He was walking too, yet who knows why he wanted to envy me.

Train

Repression is something that happens spontaneously, it's a blind visit to one's own inner universe where the gap of a missed opportunity mysteriously appears.

Chances are missed for many reasons.

Fear, for instance, is an equidistant reason, able to incinerate love. Yet, after all, love would be even more risky, so one might as well keep the fear.

Usually one can even make up traumas, and then repress them to find chances of forgiveness. Nothing can hit such a schematised individual in this sense as the understanding of a friend, who, far from blaming them, accepts even the most non-existent explanations.

When a friend forgives you, you are dead, and in the name of forgiveness you sign a mortgage with them, the usual ratified mortgage of love. At least promissory notes give a certain security; they allow you to sleep two days in a row without expecting another forfeiture. One would even commit the sin of the remainder to be forgiven. Or maybe it is an occasional way to hit people, like a delayed-action revenge?

At this point one ignores the sequences of fate. You may find yourself feeling a hand of unknown origin waking you up at 2 a.m. commanding you: 'Wake up, the train is about to leave.'

Trilogy

Once upon a time I used to be an expert of drawing; I would sit in front of an object and I would copy it with such precision and invention I was often praised for it. This virtue lasted long, then suddenly it withered in my hands: when I was about sixteen I lost the colour orientation, yet I kept a great love for painting.

That is why my house is so coloured, because I believe colour makes lifeless things look alive.

When I was little I used to know a certain Professor Lambicchi who had discovered a miraculous paint: laid on inanimate objects it would give them a body and a life, a three-dimensional life. And because three is the number of perfection, I too cultivate my trilogy: music, painting and poetry.

I believe that to make poetry you need to know not only diction and acting, but also music scales and colour. Just think that, and I know you know it; it is the sum of the colours which creates light. To see the totality of the universe then we need to take animation lessons from Professor Lambicchi.

Musical practice made me think of Amelia Rosselli, hers was such a sad life and sad death. She was a music expert too, she too secretly sang in her lieders all the tension of love she was capable of.

Was she actually being spied by the FBI or only by her genius? And wasn't this secret genius, this goblin of love, half English half French, half puritanical half sinner, Amelia's great aesthetic dualism?

Amelia… In a few days would have received the Saint Valentine award, an award which is given to all the grief-stricken lovers, to the poets who had no abode on this earth.

Yet she broke the spell that tied her to life, like that, making sure, before jumping into the void, that on the street underneath there weren't the usual tents of the beggars and that the tar was totally empty. She wanted to make sure her end would be clear as maybe her existence had not been.

Old Age

The young people that constantly travel at the edges are like light tempests, maybe a bit bothersome but so precious for the earth. With their energy they beautify our blood and carry the pride of the elders far like agile salamanders.

The elders are like meadows falling, noiselessly. They burn years of intense sacrifice in a candy wrapper. Their works won't be sold anymore: they have been many useless minions of thought.

However, when old people forget history with their mind, their wrinkles testify and remember every step taken.

They have reached tiredly the threshold of home, like wanderers with their soul suspended above them, with their hand outstretched so not to lean on the stick of your light. The elders don't want to meet their benefactors, they don't have any right to it. They are so very distant from what your path will be.

Fans

I am very hot in the summer and very cold in the winter: I am an excessive woman who doesn't love excesses. It's a dark time for me, a time where too many have seen me and too many have forgotten me.

I use fans to have my beauty baths, to soak in tepid vortexes of freshness. I love the breeze, the sea, the salty water. Yet I've only just glanced at the sea, I have always feared it, once I almost drowned in it because of love.

I have lived among those fans the whole summer in order to write, in a painless peace, looking at two neighbours of mine sleeping on the stairs. It was three of us sustaining the heat, three unlucky ladies. The most worried of us was me anyway, who, having written many books, had no money at all to go on holiday. The other two stared at me malevolently.

They both died at the end of the summer, evidently they had suffered too much. And I – the one who has been in the asylum – am still alive.

Dress

Dear little love, you are the best paper dress I have ever had, playful and deceitful like all young ones who love each other and who expel themselves out of their own body.

This house is so crossed now; the workmen have washed away all the wrinkles, all the fake smiles. And they have freshly painted the old lady, baby pink to be precise.

Do you know why you are my paper dress? Because you are like a big woollen jacket, a straightjacket. You are my madness, and you can't imagine how often madness is made solely of paper.

I write to you but I keep living here, from where you can't manage to leave, yet, because you are young, you have many departures arriving your way.

Loving you I grow without measure. I have become a vast meadow, an entire hospital, where women sick like me come and go, women sick for love. We are shapeless because of you.

Meanwhile the workmen cannot see that we, crazy for love, are dying and that, taken by such passion, we are getting old to the point that we don't ever remember we could just smile.

The crumbling house, that eye injected with silence looking at you; the labourer discussing the necessity of working around a dream. And the psychiatrist saying that people stop loving after forty.

However, the scarlet tooth of this foundry has fallen at the very best moment, when I was about to have you, when I was about to bite you. A mad desire to measure myself with you. But I can't take it anymore.

The empty house pathology has ruined me.

Neighbours

I would like to explain to you, Laura, how the woods within which the nine Muses burn are made.

Once I have perhaps suffered an unhappy freedom: within the fences of the asylum there was enough space for an impossible run, but then life arrived.

Life: a tear no one dries, an emptiness of present.

I would also like to confess to you that my language is sad because the neighbours never speak to me; they're convinced of being superior to me.

Thus, there's nothing left for me but to speak in verses, or stay mute.

And in the meantime I entangle myself in my own strength trying to become eternal.

Life

Life opens up like a mirror above us.

Lately a big comet has passed by and once again life has elapsed. And light and candour; it's an absolute novelty.

Life offers us disappointments and triumphs, punishment and tragedy. Someone may fall during this path and never raise again. They are not dead but it's like they are; some great suffering has torn them down, a deep sorrow, an unrequited love. Exactly at this point, where understanding ends, the great comet of religion begins.

Vomit

In Manganelli's *Centuria* there is a short story that portrays the poet's vomit – his inexplicable verbosity. The emphatic poet is a Don Quixote of words: he catches them like flies, he wants to align them like soldiers.

Manganelli tells that the poet, on meeting his lover after a long time, starts gently vomiting a song. And I underline 'gently', because it's a noiseless vomit, a vomit devoid of spasms of character. It's a crying dream, because the woman is sometimes a fairy, sometimes a witch, sometimes simply a lover.

In order to tell me you love me, Ernesto, you cling to the dilemma of poetry, thinking I care about the topic. Yet it isn't so: I am fed up with poetry. I would like to be a new Quasimodo.

Indeed, when I handed him *The Presence of Orpheus*[36] for the first time to get his approval, he told me, after having stared deeply into my eyes without having listened to a single word: 'Do you want to make love to me?'

This was the distracted conclusion of many feelings sung and sung again *ad nauseam* aiming at one thing only: the bed of a great poet.

---

[36] 1953 work by Merini, *La Presenza di Orfeo*, not fully translated in English. A selection of the poems contained in the book have been translated by Susan Stewart in *Love Lessons: Selected Poems by Alda Merini* (Princeton University Press, 2009) [TN].

First Conclusion

This book was supposed to be made for a theatrical transposition and such great playwright I am considering my life has been so dramatic. Yet I am also a great liar if what Manganelli says is true, i.e. that all literature is a lie.

Second Conclusion

I often wonder what a completed book leaves in one's mind. Oh, a bitter taste in your mouth for sure, and a latent despair at the thought that it might be the last song, and that the immemorial garden in ourselves can't ever be revisited again.

At the conclusion of a book one thinks of the devastating passages that have run through it, of the many conspirators who didn't want it to be born and of that ring of sky which, like Dante, closes in above our poets' halos.

You also think of the many fools who have invented you day by day and who have dictated you many topics of life, putting their angelic initials on your buttocks and often on your brain. And you understand you have been the lover of many initials.

So you close the book blissfully, leaving behind the only nail that was trying to scratch the drawing, or the relief of what could have been and isn't.

And you die once again in your foolishness, thinking you have been played once more. And sold once more like any old rag.

Thus my goodbye letter will be eternal and eternally alone like a bird. I am a migrating swallow that cannot take into account people and loved ones, who turn upside down in death.

Life calls me, poetry calls me, the same goddess who will abandon me one day. The same enemy who will declare me defeated one day.

Dis-conclusion

Yesterday Vanni Scheiwiller[37] was telling me that it's hard to talk to them who are no more.

Yet this book is a dialogue with the dead, with those who recur in the faces of the youth. Of those young people who cannot see those who still write their memories from an underground of youth.

---

[37] Italian literary critic, editor and journalist [TN].

Biography

Born in Milan on March 21st 1931, Alda Merini makes her debut in the literary world very early on: she is not even sixteen years old when Silvana Rovelli[38] shows some of her poems to Angelo Romanò[39], who, in turn, shows them to Giacinto Spagnoletti. In 1947 she meets Giorgio Manganelli, Luciano Erba[40], David Maria Turoldo[41], Maria Corti. That same year she lives through a period of intense psychological suffering.

---

[38] Cousin of the poet Ada Negri [TN].

[39] Italian writer and politician [TN].

[40] Italian poet [TN].

[41] Italian poet and priest [TN].

As Maria Corti wrote, if Manganelli has been a teacher of style for Merini, the true merit of her 'discovery' goes to Giacinto Spagnoletti, who inserted some of her poems in his *Antologia della poesia italiana* [*Anthology of Italian Poetry 1909-1949*] (Guanda, 1950)[42]. Other works of hers are published in the volume curated by Giovanni Scheiwiller *Poetesse del Novecento* [*Poetesses of the Twentieth Century*] (1951). Her first poetry book is *La presenza di Orfeo* [*The Presence of Orpheus*] (Schwarz, 1953) which, welcomed with much critical acclaim, will be republished by Vanni Schweiller in 1993 together with the next poetry collections *Paura di Dio* [*Fear of God*] (Schweiller, 1955), *Nozze romane* [*Roman Wedding*] (Schwarz, 1955), *Tu sei Pietro* [*You are Pietro*] (Schwartz, 1961). 1953 is also the year of her wedding with Ettore Carniti, owner of a number of bakeries, with whom she has her first child in 1955, a girl. Salvatore Quasimodo, to whom Merini is connected both by friendship and work, publishes some of her poems in his *Poesia italiana del dopoguerra* [*Post-War Italian Poetry*] (Schwartz, 1958).

In 1965 a very painful phase of her life begins as she gets sectioned in the psychiatric hospital Paolo Pini in Milan, where she stays till 1972. During the rare returns back home to her family she gives birth to her other three daughters.

---

[42] Those indicated in parentheses are the Italian editions.

Her poetic silence, caused among other things by her painful state of psychological distress, ends after almost twenty years, in 1979, when she begins writing some among her most intense poems, especially those collected in *La Terra Santa* [*The Holy Land*] (Scheiwiller, 1984; winner of the Cittadella Award 1985). Having lost her husband, in 1983 she marries Michele Pierri, with whom she soon moves in. Those are often difficult years, during which she comes to know the horrors of the psychiatric hospital in Taranto. Returned in Milan in 1986, she starts to publish her writings again. Memorable publications are, among others, *Fogli bianchi* [*White Sheets*] (Biblioteca Cominiana, 1987), *Testamento* [*Testament*] (Crocetti, 1988), *Vuoto d'amore* [*Vacuum of Love*] ('Poetry Collection', Einaudi, 1991) and *Ballate non pagate* [*Unpaid Ballads*] (Einaudi, 1995).

During her last year Alda Merini also dedicated herself to prose with *L'altra verità. Diario di una diversa* [*The Other Truth: Diary of a Dropout*] (Scheiwiller, 1986 and 1992; Rizzoli, 1997), *Il tormento delle figure* [*The Torment of Shapes*] (il melangolo, 1990), *Le parole di Alda Merini* [*The Words of Alda Merini*] (Stampa alternative, 1991), *Delirio amoroso* [*A Rage of Love*] (il melangolo, 1989 and 1993), *La pazza della porta accanto* [*The Crazy Woman Next Door*] (Bompiani, 1995; winner of Latina Award 1995; finalist at the Rapallo Award 1996).

In 1993 she was assigned the Librex-Guggenheim Award 'Eugenio Montale' for poetry; in 1996 she won the Viareggio Award.

Alda Merini died on the first of November 2009 in the San Paolo Hospital in Milan.